The Council of The Frick Collection
Lecture Series

J Beidelman
January 2007
New York
———

MANET'S
Incident in a Bullfight

Theodore Reff

The Council of The Frick Collection
Lecture Series

NEW YORK 2005

This publication was organized at The Frick Collection by Elaine Koss.

Dimensions are given in inches, followed by centimeters.
Height precedes width.
Design: The Oliphant Press, New York

ISBN 0-912114-28-2

PREFACE

*T*heodore Reff's "Manet's *Incident in a Bullfight*," the third of our Council Lectures to be published, is the first in the series to be devoted primarily to a work of art in the Collection itself. Henry Clay Frick acquired Manet's *Bullfight* from his preferred dealer, Knoedler's, on December 17, 1914, for the relatively modest sum of $13,500 (Degas's *Rehearsal* entered his collection at the same time). That he was fond of the picture there is no doubt, as early inventories confirm that it hung in his Sitting Room on the second floor, flanked by golfing photographs. As is well known, and as Reff eloquently demonstrates in his essay, *The Bullfight* is a fragment of a much larger work, *Incident in a Bullfight*, that Manet had shown at the Salon of 1864. The larger remnant of this Salon composition, reworked by Manet by 1867 to become *The Dead Toreador* (National Gallery of Art, Wasington), had entered the collection of Frick's great friend and fellow collector the trolley-car magnate P.A.B. Widener (1834–1907) in 1894. This was some years before Frick began to collect old masters and nineteenth-century painting in earnest, but by November 1909 portraits by Van Dyck from both collections were the subject of a small exhibition at Knoedler's gallery at 355 Fifth Avenue. And so one wonders whether the prominent display of Manet's *Dead Toreador* on a staircase wall at Lynnewood Hall, Widener's palatial residence in Elkins Park, near Philadelphia, might have encouraged Frick to make this acquisition a month and a day after his family had settled into their new residence at 1 East 70th Street.

One of a handful of the Frick's fine modern paintings from the second half of the nineteenth century, Manet's *Bullfight* has long been an admired and carefully studied work in the Collection. I am happy to acknowledge, as Reff himself does on several occasions, Susan Grace Galassi's exemplary loan exhibition and publication of 1999, *Manet's The Dead Toreador and The Bullfight: Fragments of a Lost Salon Painting Reunited*. It was at a lecture given at The Frick Collection in November 1982 that Professor Reff articulated some of the issues brought to a conclusion in his extraordinarily thorough and perceptive analysis that is published here for the first time. In thanking the author for allowing us to present, as both lecture and small book, the fruits of two decades of his thinking and research on Manet and the Bullfight, I wish also to acknowledge the meticulous and sensitive contribution of our Editor in Chief, Elaine Koss. She has shepherded the manuscript at every stage of its emergence into the handsome volume that Ron Gordon and Aaron Tilford, at The Oliphant Press, have produced for us with their customary elegance and aplomb.

Finally, I want to thank the Council of The Frick Collection for generously supporting both the lecture series that bears its name and this publication.

Colin B. Bailey
Chief Curator, The Frick Collection
December 2005

MANET'S
Incident in a Bullfight

Fig. 18. Édouard Manet, *The Dead Toreador* (detail). National Gallery of Art, Washington, D.C., Widener Collection

I realized, in trying to pull my thoughts together for this lecture, that I have been thinking about Manet's painting *Incident in a Bullfight* (fig. 1) for more than twenty years—on and off, of course, and sometimes way off. It was in 1982, in this room, that I made a first attempt to come to terms with this powerful and enigmatic work.[1] I also realized that only a little more than twenty years was the entire length of Manet's public career, from the first picture he sent to the Salon in 1859 to the last one in 1883. Yes, life is short and art is long, but art history can be even longer.

One of the reasons it has taken so much time is that the *Incident in a Bullfight* does not exist in its original form. When Manet showed the painting at the Salon of 1864, where it hung in "a place of honor,"[2] it was severely criticized and cruelly caricatured; and he later destroyed it, preserving only two fragments. In the absence of contemporary photographs, the only documentation of its original appearance is the caricatures. By definition strongly subjective, they differ in their thrust and even in their format but agree on the main features of the composition. The one by Bertall in *Le Journal amusant* (fig. 2), with its skate-boarding bull and toylike *toreros*, mocks the stiffness of the drawing and the strangeness of the perspective.[3] The cartoon by Oulevay in *Le Monde illustré* (fig. 3) adds a new charge, the schematic treatment of the arena, which becomes a domestic interior with a picture on the wall.[4] The one by Cham in *Le Charivari* (fig. 4) dwells less on the perspective than on the flatness of the strongly contrasted dark and light forms, reducing them to crudely cut-out black shapes.[5]

Of the other contemporary source, the Salon reviews, I have so far read only the eighty that seemed the most promising. They represent, incredibly enough, only about two-thirds of the number published in Paris alone.[6] It was a culture in which every newspaper and magazine, from the most established to the most marginal, felt obliged to cover the Salon, sometimes at exhausting length, as I learned during long winter hours spent squinting at microfilm in the Bibliothèque Nationale. Of those eighty reviews—of an exhibition containing more than three thousand works in all media—almost thirty had something to say about Manet's two entries.[7] This surprisingly high number no doubt reflects his notoriety after his *Luncheon on the Grass* was shown at the Salon des Refusés the year before.[8]

Only six reviews offered at least qualified approval of the *Incident in a Bullfight*, mostly of the strength and veracity of Manet's realist style—the solidity of the execution, the accuracy of the light and shadow, the authenticity of the dead figure's pose.[9] The vast majority were negative, even dismissive, outdoing each other in their sarcasm; and, reading them now, we can easily adopt the same righteous tone, thereby missing what we might learn from them. Like the cartoonists, some writers found the simplified drawing primitive. One objected to "the rigid bullfighters spaced out mechanically around the arena like fence posts."[10] Another claimed to see "a shapeless mass in the middle of the arena that is at the same time a bull, a rhinoceros, and a Paris sewer rat."[11] The ratlike bull and the horned rat were indeed frequent metaphors, expressing the writers' scorn of the wide-angle perspective, which caused the bull to appear too small in relation to the dead *toreador*. "Then there is a microscopic bull," declared one wit. "It's the perspective, you'll say. Not at all; because in the third plane, against the tiers of the arena, the *toreros* are of reasonable size and seem to be laughing at this little bull, which they could crush under the heels of their pumps."[12] Again like the cartoonists, several critics were disturbed by the powerful use of black—one of the things later artists such as Matisse most admired in Manet—and metaphors of spilled ink and black shoe polish also recurred frequently.[13] Against the black of the bull and the *toreador*'s costume, the sand of the arena was evidently a bright yellow and the barrier a reddish brown; one writer spoke of "the audacity of putting black beside yellow"[14] and another of "pallid whites and brick reds."[15] Thus the dominant colors were black, yellow, and red—the typical colors of a Spanish arena.

Surprisingly, the still more cavalier treatment of perspective and proportion in Manet's first bullfight picture, *Mlle V . . . in the Costume of an Espada* (fig. 5), had elicited no comments when he showed it at the Salon des Refusés the year before.[16] The few critics who discussed it—most were more aroused by the provocative *Luncheon on the Grass*—found other faults, but not that one. This was perhaps because the elegant and appealing *Espada* reminded them of countless tauromachian costume prints, where a *matador*, who likewise engages the spectator's eye, fills the foreground and a tiny background figure, quite out of scale, adds a Spanish accent.[17] So when its faulty perspective surfaced as the principal objection to the *Incident in a Bullfight*, Manet must have been taken aback. Evidently he took the criticism to heart,[18] for according to his lifelong friend Antonin Proust, "He boldly took a pocket knife one day and cut out the figure of the dead *toreador*."[19] That sounds rather impulsive. I hope he at least used an Exacto knife and a steel ruler; and in fact a laboratory examination has revealed carefully cut edges where the canvas was folded around a later stretcher.[20] But though Manet was certainly sensitive to criticism, and one reviewer actually suggested that he cut the picture into pieces— very small pieces, of course[21]—that was surely not his only reason. Had he agreed with the critics, he could simply have turned the large canvas upside down and painted over it, just as he had done in painting Victorine as an *espada* over a previous study of a female nude.[22] Instead, he chose to preserve and rework two fragments of the *Incident in a Bullfight* and to sign them, thus validating them as independent compositions.

A sympathetic critic, Jules Castagnary, may have encouraged Manet to do so. Castagnary objected to the lack of spatial coherence in "the *tableau* as a whole," but praised the dead *toreador* as "an excellent *morceau*."[23] As Michael Fried has shown, this distinction between the *morceau* as a piece of fine painting and the *tableau* as a coherent construction was of great interest to Realists like Castagnary in the 1860s. In Manet's own circle, Alphonse Legros was criticized for painting mere *morceaux* like Courbet's, and Fantin-Latour dreamed of creating *tableaux* like Delacroix's.[24] But Manet himself went further: cutting was merely the most extreme component of a creative process that habitually included scraping down, washing out, and painting over. This way of improvising directly on the canvas, without the traditional preliminary drawing—likened by Manet himself to learning how to swim by plunging head first into the water[25]—inaugurated what would become a familiar Modernist method.

The two paintings derived from the *Incident in a Bullfight* are the nearly life-size *Dead Toreador* (to use its conventional but outmoded title) in the National Gallery of Art (fig. 6), and the somewhat smaller *Bullfighters* in the Frick Collection (fig. 7).[26] It is now evident that both pictures were considerably reworked, indeed to such an extent that it is hard to visualize them as parts of the same composition. The sand of the arena in the background of the National Gallery picture, evidently once a bright yellow, is now a dark greenish brown; whereas in the Frick picture it is a yellowish white, played off against the reddish brown of the inner barrier and the true white of the outer one. The intensity of the light, here and in the bright blue and green costumes, suggests that it was Manet's experience of an actual bullfight, in the sunlight and shadow of the Madrid arena in September 1865, that led him to repaint the Frick fragment. It is in fact very similar in this respect to the bullfight pictures he made after his return.[27] If he had waited until then to repaint the Washington fragment, its background would probably not be the dark, opaque tone we see now, but rather the more luminous, atmospheric tone that appears in *The Fifer* and in other works inspired by the Velázquez portraits Manet had admired in the Prado.[28] But in fact he must already have reworked the *Dead Toreador* by February 1865, since he listed it among the works he planned to show in a group exhibition at the Société Nationale des Beaux-Arts that month.[29]

So Manet, the "cutter of canvases" as he has been called,[30] must have taken his knife to the *Incident in a Bullfight* in the second half of 1864, between the closing of the Salon and the preparations for the group exhibition. It probably did not figure in that show after all, but it did appear in another group exhibition, at the Cercle de l'Union Artistique, in March 1866, still bearing the title *Dead Toreador*.[31] It was only in May 1867, when he included it in the large retrospective he organized to coincide with the World's Fair, that Manet titled the picture simply *The Dead Man*, thus removing it further from its original tauromachian context and giving it a more universal significance.[32] The following year, he returned to the problem of relating the isolated figure to its field and frame by reproducing it in an etching (fig. 8). The six states, an unusually large number for Manet, show him continually adjusting the tones of the figure, the shadow, and the background.[33]

In 1982 I attempted a reconstruction of the Salon version (fig. 9), using the reviews and caricatures, biographical sources, and x-radiographs of the two fragments that were then available for the first time.[34] Recently, other scholars and conservators, including Susan Grace Galassi at the Frick and Ann Hoenigswald at the National Gallery, have proposed a more precise and complex reconstruction.[35] It confirms what I merely suggested, that Manet repainted the background even before he sent the picture to the Salon. One perceptive reviewer noted that it did not have "the freshness typical of this artist's work. It is evident that the picture has been reworked."[36]

Hoenigswald and Galassi therefore had to make two reconstructions. The first one (fig. 10) shows the composition before it was sent to the Salon,[37] with a *picador* and four minor *toreros* at the upper right and a minuscule black bull at the left. Judging from the bullfighters' actions, I think the bull was closer to and facing toward them.[38] In any event, none of these forms is now visible in the Frick picture. The second reconstruction (fig. 11) shows the composition as it probably appeared at the Salon.[39] The dead *toreador* and the three minor *toreros* largely correspond to those in the Washington and Frick canvases. The bull, who is between the minor *toreros* and the *toreador*, its head lowered as if charging, is no longer visible in the Washington picture. And in the Frick picture it is reduced to a thin black sliver, its head now raised toward the *torero* trying to provoke it. These convincing reconstructions have resolved many of my questions about the complex history of the *Incident in a Bullfight*, both before and after the Salon,[40] allowing me to turn to other equally intriguing questions.

*I*t is always assumed, first, that Manet painted the *Incident* in 1863–64 and, second, that he did so without having attended a bullfight, since he supposedly first went to Spain in 1865. But both assumptions may be wrong. Leaving aside for the moment the dating, I want to suggest that he may already have gone to Spain in 1852. Charles Limet, a distinguished lawyer and friend of the family,[41] notes in his memoirs that when he met Manet in Venice in September 1853, the young art student had already visited Spain the year before. "He came to study the Venetian masters," Limet writes, "as he had gone the year before to study in Madrid and Seville the Velázquezes, Murillos, and Goyas he was excited about."[42] Although Limet was writing many years later, his account of the time he and Manet spent in Venice is confirmed by another source.[43] Some early writers on Manet also mention or imply a trip to Spain in those early years.[44] Given his enthusiasm for Spanish art and customs, why would he not have made such a trip? It remains, however, only an intriguing and unconfirmed possibility.[45]

Equally intriguing is the possibility that Manet witnessed a bullfight in Paris. At the Combat du Taureau, a makeshift outdoor arena in the Belleville district, animal fights had been held since 1778, including on occasion "bullfights in the Spanish style, . . . followed by the slaying of a bull by *toreros*, the way this spectacle is performed in Spain."[46] Repeatedly shut down by the police and repeatedly reopened for commercial gain, this notorious establishment continued to present animal fights, though not necessarily between men and bulls, until about 1850.[47] In that year, the so-called Loi Grammont was passed, prohibiting cruelty to domestic and farm animals and, in the case of bullfights, requiring the bulls' horns to be capped, the *toreros* to carry no weapons, and the horses, who were always the first victims, to be excluded.[48] In effect, a kind of taurine ballet was to be performed, to avoid offending the moral values of the increasingly powerful middle class and the increasingly influential intelligentsia. The campaign to pass the law, led by the recently formed Société Protectrice des Animaux, was supported by politically liberal writers such as Jules Michelet and Victor Hugo, in the face of fierce conservative opposition.[49]

That opposition remained so great that enforcement of the Loi Grammont, some of whose clauses were ambiguous, often required negotiation and compromise. Some such arrangement was presumably what permitted the performance in Paris of a bullfight that Courbet must have seen before he made a painting about 1855 (fig. 12) that shows a *picador* and four *toreros* trying to distract the bull from attacking a fifth one lying on the ground.[50] I have found no program and only one review of such an event; yet the setting is so specific—the old Hippodrome near the Champs-Élysées, with the Arc de Triomphe visible in the background[51]—that it is hard to imagine the great Realist inventing the whole thing. In any case, what we see in this curious little picture is a French form of bullfight, despite the mounted *picador* at the right. That such an event did take place at the Hippodrome in this period is

14

evident from a newspaper review published in August 1849 by Théophile Gautier, who, like a true *aficionado*, regretted only the limitations imposed by French custom.[52]

Even if Manet had seen a Spanish *corrida* in Madrid or Paris about 1850, his memory of it would have been faint when he began more than a decade later to envisage the *Incident in a Bullfight*. But more recently he may have seen, if not a bullfight, then Spanish bullfighters. The journal *Le Monde dramatique* reported in October 1862 that a group of them had been authorized to perform at the new Hippodrome, built at the Rond-Point de Saint-Cloud after the old one burned down.[53] It is very unlikely that authorization would have been given, and I have found no other mention of a performance in the press or in the Paris police archives. But given Manet's enthusiasm at the time for everything Spanish, he may well have invited the group to visit his studio, or the more presentable studio of his friend Alfred Stevens, just as he did when Lola de Valence's troupe of Spanish dancers performed at the Hippodrome from August to October 1862.[54] A likely result of such a visit is the painting traditionally titled *The Inn* (fig. 13), which shows bullfighters standing about or praying before an image of the Virgin, as was their custom before entering the arena.[55] Typically for Manet, his image of such a scene is based as much on graphic models—etchings by Goya, a lithograph by Pharamond Blanchard, his own etching after Velázquez—as on direct observation.[56]

It was only in 1865, well after he exhibited the *Incident in a Bullfight* at the Salon, that Manet could definitely have witnessed a bullfight in Paris. A group of Spanish *toreros* was finally allowed to perform at the Hippodrome in August and September, but with so many restrictions imposed by the Loi Grammont,[57] that the public's initial enthusiasm soon changed to scornful ridicule. Triple-Diable, one of the dangerous bulls featured on the huge posters, turned out to be a small, mild creature who, rather than attack his opponents, made a graceful tour of the arena like a circus horse.[58]

Ironically, at that very moment in early September 1865 Manet himself was in Madrid, attending a real bullfight. He had made the trip primarily to visit the Prado, but his friend Zacharie Astruc had advised him also to witness a *corrida*.[59] Like other French visitors who in principle were opposed to the violent spectacle but in practice were fascinated by its dramatic intensity, Manet was enthusiastic. "One of the finest, most curious and most terrifying sights to be seen," he wrote to Baudelaire, "is a bullfight. When I get back, I hope to put down on canvas the brilliant, glittering effect and also the drama of the *corrida* I saw."[60] A few days later, he wrote to Astruc that he wanted to capture "the colorful crowd, and the dramatic aspect as well, the *picador* and horse overturned, with the bull's horns plowing into them and the horde of minor *toreros* trying to draw the furious beast away."[61] The paintings he made on his return to Paris (figs. 14, 15) show that he had not forgotten either the colorful or the dramatic part of the spectacle.[62]

*A*ssuming that in 1862–64 Manet had not yet witnessed a Spanish bull-fight, he was obliged to imagine one, and he therefore turned to both visual and textual sources. Antonin Proust tells us that Manet had long admired Alfred Dehodencq's *Village Bullfight in Spain* (fig. 16), which was shown at the Salon of 1850, bought by the State, and installed in the museum of contemporary art in Paris, where Manet and his friends Astruc, Fantin-Latour, and Alphonse Legros studied it closely.[63] An etched copy was also available, as were a great many other prints on tauromachian subjects in this period of *espagnolisme* in all the arts.[64] Typical of this imagery are a suite of colored lithographs by Pharamond Blanchard, issued in 1852,[65] and wood engravings after drawings by Gustave Doré (e.g., fig. 17) illustrating a travel article of 1862.[66] But their emphasis on sheer spectacle and their relatively small formats set them apart from Manet's monumental painting, in which violence and local color have been transformed into stillness and somber elegy, and the dominant colors are black and white.[67]

Clearly, prints like Blanchard's and Doré's were not what led Manet to conceive his bullfight in such stark, dramatic terms. Nor was it a painting he saw at the Salon; the only bullfight pictures shown there since 1850—and their virtual absence is another indication of the singularity of Manet's picture—likewise dwelled on the theatrical rather than the tragic aspect of the subject.[68] I think it was a text rather than a picture that inspired him, a newspaper account of the death of a *matador* in the Madrid bullring. In the issue of April 30, 1862, of *Le Siècle*, a paper whose editor he knew and whose republican politics he shared[69]—that's lower-case republican, you understand—Manet could have read the following article, datelined Madrid, April 24:

At this moment, the public's attention is entirely absorbed by the

deplorable accident that occurred on April 21st at the *corrida* that inaugurated the spring season. An unfortunate *matador*, one of the premier
swordsmen of Madrid, José Rodriguez, known by the nickname of
Pepete, was killed on the spot by a bull. . . . The superb animal, elegant
and nervous in form, had made a magnificent entry. After having sur-
veyed the arena and the audience, it darted like an arrow at the *picador*
Antonio Calderon, lifted on its head the man and his horse, and threw
them both on the ground. At this moment Pepete saw the imminent dan-
ger of the *picador*. More concerned with the salvation of his companion
than with his own safety, the brave and generous young man ran to him.
Unfortunately the bull, one of the most dangerous in its agility that has
ever been seen, spotted its adversary and, with a leap as fast as lightning,
attacked him. It struck him on the hip, passed one of its horns under his
ribs and, balancing him for a few seconds above its head, finished by giving him a furious thrust of the horn, which penetrated one lung and his
heart. After that it left its victim stretched out on the ground. Pepete
raised himself with great difficulty, brought his right hand to his face as if
to wipe away the sweat, then placed it over his heart.[70]

It is no coincidence, then, that Manet imagined his *toreador* making just
this gesture before expiring, or that the spots of blood on his shirt and right
hand and the pool of blood at his shoulder all indicate a wound in his chest
and back. Nor is it a coincidence that the *toreador*'s features are distinctly
Spanish (fig. 18), presumably those of the dancer in Lola de Valence's troupe
who is reported to have posed for Manet.[71] But it probably *is* a coincidence
that they also resemble, even when seen in this foreshortened view, the features of Pepete himself, which were known from contemporary photographs
(e.g., fig. 19).[72]

The event produced a great outpouring of newspaper and magazine articles, of poems and songs celebrating Pepete's heroism.[73] Dignified portraits
like the photograph in figure 19 and poignant scenes like the anonymous wash
drawing of his fatal injury, showing him caught on the bull's horns and hoist-
ed over its head (fig. 20),[74] were widely circulated. And perhaps more important for Manet, they circulated in the form of photographs. Jean Laurent, who
had shops in Paris and Madrid, was already offering for sale in 1863 some fifty
photographs of tauromachian subjects, among them portraits of Pepete and

this very drawing.[75] Whether or not Manet also relied on such documents for the *Incident in a Bullfight*, as he did for his later bullfight paintings,[76] I think the graphic account in *Le Siècle* of Pepete's death must have been his point of departure.

One reason for thinking so is that Manet would soon rely on illustrated newspaper stories for information and imagery in painting other topical events he had not witnessed firsthand. He did so in the spring of 1864 to depict an episode in the American Civil War, the naval battle of the Confederacy's *Alabama* and the Union's *Kearsarge* off the coast of Cherbourg. For despite his friend Proust's vivid report of Manet observing the battle from a small boat, there is no evidence that he ever visited Cherbourg.[77] He relied again on newspapers in the summer and fall of 1867 to represent the tragic end of Napoleon III's Mexican campaign, the execution of the emperor Maximilian at Querétaro, revising and refining his depiction as additional accounts and photographs gradually became available, though he clearly did not follow them literally.[78]

The speeches and memorial poems on Pepete's death dwelt on the fact that his was the first death to occur in the Madrid arena since that of José Delgado, better known as Pepe-Hillo, sixty-one years earlier.[79] Many other *toreros* were of course killed in the interim, but not in the premier arena of Madrid. And just as the death of Pepete was, if I am right, the implicit subject of Manet's *Incident in a Bullfight*, so the death of Pepe-Hillo was explicitly the subject of the culminating work in Goya's *Art of Bullfighting* etchings (fig. 21).[80] One reviewer of the Salon of 1864 remarked on the affinities between Manet's bullfight scene and Goya's prints, with which we know he was familiar.[81] Another reviewer, the well-informed Hispanophile Gautier, specified that "A similar motif was treated by Goya in the Death of Pepe Hillo, the celebrated swordsman."[82] In choosing this subject, then, Manet may well have been presenting himself as the Goya of his own time. The critics did not fail to respond, finding affinities between Manet's strangely imagined, boldly simplified, and intensely colored painting and the ones they knew, or knew about, by his equally eccentric predecessor.[83]

*T*here is a more fundamental analogy between Goya's print and Manet's painting. Both works can be seen as expressing revulsion against the Spanish form of bullfighting and support for contemporary campaigns to suppress or modify its violence. The *Art of Bullfighting* etchings, satirizing the coarseness and cruelty of participants and spectators alike, reflects the liberal, enlightened criticism of the national sport that was common in Goya's circle in the very years when he worked on the series.[84] In the same way, the *Incident in a Bullfight* condemns a barbaric practice that was not congenial to French custom and was in fact contrary to French law, though it remained an integral part of local culture in the south of France, and during the Second Empire became more popular even in the north.[85] This was despite the continual efforts of the Society for the Protection of Animals, founded in 1846, to call attention to the inhumanity of bullfighting and to the injuries and deaths it caused. In May 1863, when Manet was presumably still working on his painting, the Society published a tract documenting all such incidents in France and Spain, and again linking the deaths of Pepete and Pepe Hillo.[86]

Its author, Dr. Henri Blatin, was a pediatrician and gynecologist who, before becoming vice-president of the Society, had sought ways to make childbirth safer and less painful and had founded an organization to protect the rights of children. Not surprisingly, he and the co-founder of the Society, Dr. Pierre Dumont (de Monteux), were staunch republicans.[87] But can we assume that Manet shared their views on bullfighting as well as their political views? In a few years, he would be fascinated by the *corridas* he saw in Madrid, and would depict a bull goring a horse as energetically as he depicted the colorful crowd and arena. How can we reconcile these pictures with the tragic view of bullfighting he painted only a few years earlier? One way, I think, is to recognize that the later works, of modest dimensions and fluently executed, were made to record a vivid personal experience, whereas the earlier work, larger in scale, extensively reworked, and powerful even if awkward in construction, was meant to make an ambitious public statement. It was in fact the first bullfight painting by a French artist to appear at the Salon since Dehodencq's in 1850, and even that had depicted the playfulness of a *novillada*, not the violence of a true *corrida*.[88]

Another way, equally important, is to realize that Manet was not unusual among people who shared his liberal, secular views in condemning the Spanish bullfight, while nevertheless finding it visually and emotionally fascinating. Here is how an influential republican ideologue, the philosopher Ernest Bersot, struggles to reconcile his aesthetic and moral positions.[89] He begins with the official stance: "I have no desire for bullfighting to be established in France: the sight of blood is bad." But with admirable honesty, as the scholar he is of Rousseau and Voltaire, Bersot goes on to describe the "savage, virile, powerful spectacle" he saw in Madrid. And although he condemns the evisceration of the horses, he lucidly notes that "soon one no longer sees it. The art inherent in tragedy grips you, absorbs you, and the rest recedes more and more into the shadows and disappears."[90] This, it seems to me, is exactly how Manet would have reconciled his conflicting values.

Manet too, of course, held strongly republican views, having grown up with them. Charles Limet, whose memoirs I quoted earlier, recalled that he had first met Manet's father in December 1851, while both were recoiling at the closing of a courthouse during the *coup d'état* that would soon make Louis Napoleon emperor.[91] On the same day, Manet himself narrowly escaped a cavalry charge sweeping the streets of potential protesters; and a few days later he visited the Montmartre cemetery to view the victims.[92] His brother Gustave was to become a liberal lawyer, a representative of a working-class district, and president of the radicalized Municipal Council of Montmartre. Growing up in this milieu, Manet was already writing to his father on an ocean voyage in 1849, "Try to preserve our good republic until my return, for I well and truly fear that Louis Napoleon is not himself much of a republican."[93] Later, he frequented radical cafés and salons, became a close friend of the republican politician Léon Gambetta, whose portrait he wanted to paint, and of the ex-Communard Henri Rochefort, whose portrait he did paint, capturing perfectly his defiant stance;[94] and at the opposite end of the political spectrum, he caricatured the reactionary president Patrice MacMahon as an insolent Punchinello, half martinet, half buffoon.[95]

For secular republicans like Manet and Bersot, animal and human life were stages in a continual evolutionary process, and all life deserved to be protected and prolonged. Hence their opposition to the killing of horses and bulls as well as men in the Spanish *corrida*. For orthodox conservatives like Louis Veuillot, on the contrary, animals were distinctly inferior to humans and destined only to serve them, and even human death could be accepted in the larger Catholic perspective of eternal life.[96] Hence their approval of the ritual killings in the symbolic drama of life and death that was enacted in a true *corrida*. The opposed positions were epitomized by two of the foremost Romantic writers. To Théophile Gautier, a Spanish bullfight was a "struggle in which the rational courage of man grapples with the blind force of beasts, one whose importance exceeds that of every conceivable tragedy."[97] To Victor Hugo, it was merely a mindless, sadistic sport; and his condemnation has been cited by animal rights activists ever since: "Killing a bull for the pleasure, for the amusement, is much more than torturing an animal, it is torturing a conscience."[98]

*I*nevitably, in Second Empire France, the debate had a political as well as an ideological dimension. Whereas Gautier became a favorite at court and its quasi-official poet and chronicler of cultural events, Hugo was forced into exile in Brussels, where he published devastating critiques like *Les Châtiments* and *Napoléon le Petit*. Appropriately, it was in the pages of *Le Siècle*, an opposition newspaper, that the article on Pepete's death appeared, concluding with the observation that "a very vivid movement of reaction against the savage pleasure of the bullfight" was emerging in Spain.[99] The movement did not in fact remain vivid for long; and even in France it could make little progress under the imperial regime. Indeed the force behind the introduction of the Spanish form of bullfighting into France was the Empress Eugénie herself (fig. 22), a devoutly Catholic Spanish aristocrat with a passion for the national sport.

In September 1852, only months before Eugénie married Napoleon III, a troupe of Spanish *toreros* was permitted to perform in a new arena at Saint-Esprit, just outside Bayonne, a city near the Spanish border with a sporadic history of bullfights.[100] During summer vacations thereafter, the imperial couple attended frequently, and the pomp and circumstance of their ceremonial entrances and ritual exchanges with the *toreros* were widely reported in both the local and the international press.[101] The beautiful Eugénie even persuaded the infatuated Napoleon to build a vacation villa—named of course Villa Eugénie—a short distance away at Biarritz, which launched that city's fame as a seaside resort. And he was shrewd enough to realize that authorizing Spanish bullfights in southern cities—the example of Bayonne was soon followed at Arles, Nîmes, and elsewhere—would help him to maintain popular support in the south for his increasingly unpopular regime.

Eugénie had been an *aficionada* since her earliest days in Madrid as a socialite given to unconventional behavior. She enjoyed making sensational entrances into the stands and presiding over the awarding of prizes. She flirted with and invited to her home celebrated *toreros* such as El Chichanero, with whom it was rumored she had an affair.[102] Such was her reputation in some quarters that the anonymous author of *Les Femmes galantes des Napoléons*, published in London in 1862, could claim that El Chichanero was but one of many victorious *toreros* to be accorded her favors, and that the bullfight itself was for her a voluptuous pleasure in violence that reached its paroxysm when one of the *toreros* fell.[103] Here, in the very year in which Manet began his *Incident in a Bullfight*, the regime's infatuation with bullfighting was being used, however unscrupulously, as a metaphor for its moral debasement.

Is there a hint of that image of Eugénie in Manet's painting of Victorine as an *espada*, which otherwise seems so implausible, as if she were entering a costume ball at the Tuileries palace rather than a bullring in Madrid? The out-of-scale bullfight in the background, based on another of Goya's *Art of Bullfighting* etchings (fig. 23), only enhances the contrived, theatrical effect.[104] The piece of salmon-colored fabric Victorine holds, which an x-radiograph reveals she originally held in both hands, without a sword,[105] functions primarily as a fashion accessory, like her shiny silk hose. And the rest of her costume, the black velvet bolero and tight black breeches, which Manet owned and used in painting other Spanish subjects, is more like that of a Spanish mule driver.[106] That he knew perfectly well from tauromachian costume prints and from the travel writings of Gautier, Alexandre Dumas, and others what a *matador*'s elaborate and colorful costume looked like is clear from his portrait of the Spanish dancer Mariano Camprubi wearing such a costume (fig. 24), which likewise dates from 1862.[107]

Victorine's appearance in male attire and in playing a distinctly male role would also have suited Eugénie perfectly. The sexual ambiguity of the picture, which even led some contemporaries to call it *Le Toréador*,[108] would have pointed to just those masculine traits that were cited by the radical opposition as proof of Eugénie's dominant role in the government. The malicious author of *Les Femmes galantes* was certain that she had always had such inclinations, excelling in men's sports, often dressing as a man, and smoking cigarettes and cigars; in short, that she "handled the dagger better than the fan."[109] She seems especially to have enjoyed cross-dressing as a gypsy and a smuggler—and also as a bullfighter. A watercolor of 1852 (fig. 25), the year before she married Napoleon, shows her returning from a *corrida* in the south of Spain, astride her horse like a man, and wearing a bullfighter's *bolero* and *montera*.[110] Cross-dressing, it is true, was a form of feminist assertiveness at the time, and Eugène Disdéri's photographs of dancers and singers dressed as *toreros*, including one published in 1861 (fig. 26), may have been familiar to Manet.[111] Moreover, there was a long tradition in the Spanish bullring of actual *señoritas toreras*, one of whom appears, posing triumphantly over a dead bull, in a print by Gustave Doré.[112] But such images would only have reinforced in Manet's mind the image of Eugénie already prevalent in his republican circle.[113]

*I*f the *Incident in a Bullfight* can thus be seen as an allusion to the decadent moral values of the Second Empire, it can also be seen as an attack on one of its major international actions, the invasion of Mexico in 1862 to effect a regime change. Eugénie, who later boasted of her role in the affair, had long sought to replace the liberal republic of Benito Juárez with an authoritarian empire that would restore the power of the landed aristocracy, the allies of the Spanish Carlists, and the Catholic Church.[114] While sharing these motives, Napoleon had important ones of his own: among others, to compensate French companies for the huge financial losses incurred by Juárez's defaults on foreign loans; to halt and even reverse the expansion of American economic and political power in the hemisphere; to achieve his goal of creating a Franco-Austrian alliance by installing the Archduke Maximilian as emperor; and to realize his vision of a Latin empire embracing the Mediterranean lands and their former possessions in what would henceforth be called Latin America.[115] In this imperial regime, the motives of one powerful figure were largely economic and political, those of the other largely ideological; and we know what a lethal mixture that can be.

The decision to invade was taken at Biarritz in September 1861, during secret meetings closed even to high government officials. But one outsider was present: José Hidalgo, a Mexican diplomat living in Europe. Well connected, self-serving, and suave, a kind of Ahmad Chalabi *avant la lettre*, Hidalgo had insinuated himself into Eugénie's favor and, with other reactionary *émigrés*, had schemed with her for regime change in Mexico.[116] The French army, then the most powerful in the world, would triumph decisively, the people would receive it with open arms, and so on in a litany all too familiar today. The weak but dynastically ambitious Maximilian was persuaded, with a promise of continued French military support, to assume the Mexican throne. But faced with mounting human and financial losses, increasingly outspoken disapproval at home, and the growing threat of American intervention, Napoleon eventually had to withdraw, abandoning Maximilian to his fate. Betrayed by a trusted officer in his final stand at Querétaro, Maximilian was defeated, and he and his generals were executed by a Mexican firing squad in June 1867. When the news reached France in July, Manet reacted strongly, undertaking a large, energetic painting, then three more paintings, increasingly refined and precise—the final one is at Mannheim (fig. 27)—as well as a lithograph intended to disseminate the image more widely.[117]

As has often been noted, Manet conceived the execution in terms of a bullfight, a ceremonial death at close quarters in an arena with spectators.[118] The Mexican setting was appropriate, since Mexican bullfighting was as popular as Spanish bullfighting and was thought to surpass it in brilliance.[119] Appropriately, too, bullfighting had been encouraged by Maximilian and the conservatives who installed him, just as it would be suppressed, despite its continued popularity, when Juárez and the liberals regained power in 1867.[120] The firing squad in Manet's final version, too close to the victims to be realistic, evokes the *matador* standing close to the bull in one of his 1865 paintings; and the wall behind them recalls the barrier of the arena. The Mexican peasants peering over the wall call to mind the Spanish spectators looking over the barrier in some of Goya's *Art of Bullfighting* etchings.[121] And just as the bulls in Goya's prints may symbolize, as Janis Tomlinson has argued, the popular resistance to Napoleon the First's campaign to conquer Spain,[122] so the dead *toreador* in the *Incident in a Bullfight* may symbolize the victims of his nephew's attempt to subjugate Mexico.

There are further reasons to think that the *Incident in a Bullfight* evokes the Mexican campaign. As we have seen, a *matador's* costume would normally be colorful and elaborately embroidered. He would wear black only if he were in mourning for a close relative,[123] but in any event it would not be the black costume of Manet's dead *toreador*. When he dressed his model Victorine in the same costume as an *espada*, the result was quite different: the black bolero and breeches, enlivened by colored scarves, looked up-to-date and chic, as if black were the color that summer. On the dead *toreador* it is not only funereal, but also disturbingly similar to the uniform of contemporary French soldiers. With its dominant black marked by accents of white at the waist and feet, it is like the uniform of the firing squad in the *Execution of the Emperor Maximilian*, a more explicit indictment of the disastrous Mexican campaign.

The *Incident in a Bullfight* can thus be seen as alluding to recent French losses: the eight hundred killed, wounded, or missing in the humiliating defeat at Puebla in May 1862—the legendary Cinco de Mayo—and the hundreds more killed at Camarón and elsewhere by the unexpectedly fierce resistance and above all by tropical diseases.[124] When news of the Puebla defeat reached Paris a month later, despite government censorship, there was a vociferous public reaction; and criticism of this latest imperial adventure appeared in the opposition newspapers, in speeches during legislative debates, and even in the reports of Napoleon's agents in the provinces.[125] Republicans like Manet, who had opposed the imperialist campaign from the beginning, had fresh reasons to condemn it. When heavily reinforced French troops retook Puebla a year later after a long siege and went on to take Mexico City, both military pride and public confidence were restored, but the war continued to take its toll and to require thousands more to be sent abroad. It was at just this time and in this political milieu that Manet painted and planned to show at the Salon his *Incident in a Bullfight*.

But in fact, how do we know when he painted it? The date always given, 1863–64, is a result of counting back from the opening of the Salon in May 1864, but why stop counting there? Manet could withhold a picture from exhibition for years, as is evident from the case of *Olympia*, painted in 1862–63 and first shown at the Salon of 1865. There are reasons to think that the *Incident in a Bullfight* dates from the second half of 1862 and the first of 1863, a time when Manet was completely absorbed in Spanish subjects—in fact, the only time before he went to Spain in 1865. Adolphe Tabarant, the first modern cataloguer of his work, states flatly that in the summer or fall of 1862 Manet "began an *Episode in a Bullfight* that did not satisfy him and that he abandoned, took up again, and still could not finalize," and that in the winter of 1864, while preparing for the upcoming Salon, he returned to it once more.[126] He was indeed so pressed for time to complete his submissions to the Salon that he had to petition for an extension of the deadline.[127] As we have seen, the x-radiographs reveal extensive revisions made even before Manet showed the picture at the Salon. And the two events that seem to have inspired him, the death of Pepete and the defeat at Puebla, both occurred in the spring of 1862.

The battles at Puebla and elsewhere in Mexico were of such current importance that we may wonder why they were not treated by other artists, if not allusively then overtly, like so many of Napoleon's other battles, from Sebastopol to Solferino. In fact they *were* treated: the specialist in battle scenes Jean-Adolphe Beaucé was embedded in the French expeditionary force in central Mexico in 1863–65, collecting material for several pictures he had been commissioned to paint, including the second Battle of Puebla.[128] But the scale of these works was so large, and their subjects so complex, that Beaucé completed them only several years later, and showed them at Salons in the late 1860s, by which time of course the news was cold.[129] The rarity of such pictures at the Salon of 1864, when the news was still hot, was noted by the critic for the *Revue militaire*. "On entering the exhibition," he wrote, "I thought I was going to see the walls covered with the battles waged from Puebla to Mexico City, but there was nothing of the sort."[130] How he overlooked a large, prominently displayed painting by Janet-Lange of the Battle of Altesco[131] is hard to understand—harder perhaps than how he also overlooked Manet's *Incident in a Bullfight*.

I am not the only one to suspect that this picture alludes to the first act of the tragedy whose final act is shown in the *Execution of the Emperor Maximilian*. Wilson-Bareau has raised the same possibility; and while denying that the *Incident in a Bullfight* is strictly speaking "an allegory of the events in Mexico," she adds: "It would be very remarkable if such a politically alert and independent artist did not take account of these events."[132] But is there any evidence that Manet's contemporaries understood the picture in such terms? The most likely place to look is in reviews of the Salon of 1864, which is of course one of the reasons I spent so much time squinting at microfilm. But the only review I found that hints at a political subtext is the one that Wilson-Bareau also cites, published in *L'Indépendance belge* by Théophile Thoré.[133] Thoré was, it is true, the most visually astute critic of this period and also the most politically radical, having spent a decade in exile for his role in the 1848 revolution. But if, as we would expect, he strongly condemns Napoleon's encouragement of bullfighting in France, he says nothing about the war in Mexico.[134] It is only the context in which he discusses the picture that leads Wilson-Bareau to speculate that Thoré, like Manet himself, meant more than he said.

By discussing them back to back, Thoré implicitly links the *Incident in a Bullfight* with another picture shown at the Salon of 1864, Désiré Laugée's

Episode in the Polish Wars in 1863, which Thoré calls "a terrible argument against violent repressions."[135] The insurrection against the Czar in the Russian part of Poland and its ruthless suppression aroused a great deal of sympathy in France, as well as criticism of Napoleon for cynically remaining aloof while trying to impose an equally repressive regime on Mexico.[136] Laugée's picture is no longer extant, but it is clear from the reviews that its principal figure, a slain woman looming large in the foreground, was analogous to Manet's *toreador*.[137] Seizing on this resemblance, Thoré describes "the naked, battered corpse of this beautiful and noble young woman," then says of Manet's *toreador*: "Here is another victim of the viciousness of public morals, disemboweled for the amusement of several thousand overwrought spectators." Can we infer from this sequence, from Laugée and Poland to Manet and Spain/Mexico, that Thoré is also linking the regime's enthusiasm for this brutal spectacle with the ruthlessness of its foreign policy? That seems rather circuitous; and I wonder why Thoré, writing under a pseudonym and for a Belgian newspaper, would not have taken a more direct route, as Victor Hugo and other political exiles did in attacking the regime. For Manet himself, however, the circuitous route was probably the only one available.

If he did intend to paint an ambitious Salon picture to make a political statement, it could only be in the form of an allusion; otherwise, it would surely have been rejected, just as his *Execution of the Emperor Maximilian* would later be rejected, as he was led to understand, if he submitted it to the Salon.[138] Living under an autocratic regime so fearful of the power of images that its restrictions revealed what has been called "a sensitivity that verged on paranoia,"[139] Manet probably had no choice but to resort to allusion. And if I can count on a New York audience to understand my allusions to the current war in Iraq, why couldn't Manet count on a Parisian audience to understand his allusions to the then-current war in Mexico? For Thoré, and for much enlightened French opinion, Mexico and Poland represented equally dismal foreign policy failures. Thus he could compare the victims of a savage repression Napoleon did nothing to stop with the victims of a savage sport he did everything to promote. And though Manet was not Thoré, I think he could make essentially the same point in his own inherently less rhetorical medium—and could do so even in choosing his pictorial models.

$\mathcal{A}$rt historians have long recognized that the principal model for the dead *toreador* is a picture of a dead soldier that was then attributed to Velázquez (fig. 28), one of the old masters Manet most admired, and that was then known as the *Orlando muerto*.[140] Like the *toreador*, the dead soldier is clad in stark black and white, within a setting of greenish browns, and lies facing to the left on a diagonal axis, his right hand on his chest. But his left arm is bent, still holding his sword, and his head faces resolutely forward—differences which, with the smoking lamp above him and the skull and bones beside him, give his death an otherworldly rather than a mundane connotation.[141] The strong similarities in physical size and scale of the two figures and in their relation to the frame and the surrounding space suggest that Manet may also have recalled the *Orlando muerto* in formatting the fragment he created from the larger work.[142]

The connection was already recognized by the first art historians to write about the *Incident in a Bullfight*. When it was shown at the Salon, Gautier suspected that "the warm muffled black tones of the *matador's* garments were borrowed from Velasquez' palette."[143] Thoré was more specific, calling the *toreador* "a life-size figure audaciously copied from a masterpiece in the Pourtalès Collection, assuredly painted by Velázquez."[144] Baudelaire, writing privately to Thoré a few days later, defended his friend Manet against the charge of plagiarism: "The word 'imitation' is unfair," he wrote. "Manet has never seen the Pourtalès Collection. This seems unbelievable to you, but it's true."[145] Thoré, in a reply published along with Baudelaire's letter, insisted that Manet must have seen the Velázquez, if not in the original, then in a reproduction, and he recalled that a photograph had been published recently.[146] Here the sober art historian trumped the impassioned poet: the Pourtalès Collection, one of the most important in Europe, was open one day a week to qualified visitors;[147] and the photograph Thoré mentions was evidently published in January 1863.[148]

In their search for Manet's models, art detectives have discovered other cadavers, notably the *Dead Caesar* by the successful academic artist Jean-Léon Gérôme. Widely admired at the Salon of 1859, but sold a century later for the frame alone and presumably destroyed, it is now known only from a photograph taken at the time (fig. 29).[149] Obviously Gérôme's figure faces in the opposite direction from the dead *toreador*, but it is laid out on the same diagonal with its feet extending at exactly the same angles, one of its arms is outstretched, and its head is turned to the side. And like the *toreador* in its original context, the figure looms dramatically in the foreground of a deep space, which of course is constructed in correct perspective.

When the *Dead Caesar* was shown at the Salon, several critics realized what you have just realized, that it too is based on the *Orlando muerto*.[150] We know that Gérôme had visited the Pourtalès Collection to study its celebrated antiquities.[151] But the critics also noted that Caesar, largely concealed beneath his voluminous, elaborately folded toga, failed to evoke the same sensation of death: "The drapery that covers the corpse," one of them wrote, "also covers our feelings."[152] The same cannot be said of Manet's *toreador*, which I think surpasses both the *Caesar* and the *Orlando* in expressing, through its form and color as well as its subject, the inexorable nature of death.

Just as Manet produced a second version of his bullfight picture by reducing the colorful action scene to the still figure of the dead *toreador*, so Gérôme painted a second version of his Caesar picture, now called *The Death of Caesar* (fig. 30), by enlarging its scope to include more of the carefully reconstructed Theater of Pompey, the triumphant conspirators departing, and an old senator unaware of what has occurred.[153] In short, Gérôme expanded his image into a historical epic, whereas Manet concentrated his into a terse elegy. It was just this concentration that Baudelaire had admired in Gérôme's first version: "It was indeed a happy moment," Baudelaire wrote, "when he conceived his Caesar alone, stretched out in front of his overturned throne. . . . This terrible summary is enough."[154] Did Manet have in mind these words, by the writer who meant more to him than any other, when he too finally conceived his *toreador* alone? Whether he did or not, by reducing the larger composition to the single figure, he restored its visual relationship to the putative Velázquez and evoked its thematic relationship, as an image of a modern hero's death, to the deaths of an ancient and a medieval hero.

As if all that were not enough, there is another dead man lurking in the literature on Manet, this one interred there by Beatrice Farwell.[155] He is neither a knight nor an emperor, but a lowly robber, who has been killed in an armed attack on a stagecoach on a country road. Not immediately visible in the composition (fig. 31), he lies at the lower left in the now-familiar pose, his left arm extended and holding his rifle, his head fallen to the left, while the assault rages on behind him. The drawing, illustrating an episode in Alain Lesage's popular novel *Gil Blas de Santillane*, was made by Jean Gigoux for an

1835 deluxe edition.[156] Gigoux's lively illustrations were much admired, among others by the young Édouard Manet, according to his friend Antonin Proust, who adds that Manet used the frontispiece as a model for an earlier painting.[157] Given this reassuring information, and the striking visual evidence—Gigoux's dead robber could play the dead *toreador* more convincingly than any of our other tryouts for the part—perhaps we should accept him as Manet's real model and be done with it.

Unfortunately, we can't do that. If the dead *toreador*, the dead Caesar, and the dead knight are all nearly life size, the dead robber—though you would never know it from the images you see here—is only about the length of one of their thumbs. A tiny image compared to the others, it would hardly have had the same impact on Manet or remained so clearly in his memory. And equally important, the foreshortened pose of Gigoux's figure is, as W. S. Heckscher has noted, "a common and ages-old device by which a prone body can serve to express the suffering, surrender, and passivity in general of the defenseless, the dying, and the dead."[158] As such it appears in high art and popular art—the dead mother in Poussin's much-admired *Plague at Ashdod*, which Manet had surely seen in the Louvre, and the fallen general in an Épinal print celebrating the recapture of Puebla (fig. 32), to which Wilson-Bareau has called attention.[159] Both figures, prominently placed in the foreground, lie in exactly the same diagonal position as the dead *toreador* in Manet's painting. And as a piece of widely circulated propaganda, the Épinal print published in June 1863 was a more likely source for Manet to have seen and used than the *Gil Blas* illustration published almost twenty years earlier, and one whose subject was more relevant.

*T*hat, I think, is the crucial issue: the two paintings that Manet seems most to have relied on in conceiving his *Incident in a Bullfight* were meaningful in their subjects as well as their forms. The *Dead Soldier* was known at the time as *Orlando muerto* (the *Dead Roland*). This was just as incorrect as the attribution to Velázquez, since the picture is a kind of traditional "vanitas," in which a dead warrior, a symbol of Christian valor, is flanked by a skull and bones and a lamp with a smoking wick, symbols of death and the vanity of human striving.[160] But the title has become established in the Manet literature, and art historians keep repeating the name, as if Orlando Muerto were a real person, perhaps the older brother of the second baseman José Muerto. In fact, he is the legendary Roland, the hero of the *Chanson de Roland*, the eleventh-century poem that has been revered since the Middle Ages as the national epic, the French equivalent of the *Iliad*.

A nephew of Charlemagne's, Roland commands the rear guard of the Frankish army returning across the Pyrenees from its invasion of Spain. Through the treachery of his stepfather, Ganelon, Roland's forces are trapped in a mountain pass and annihilated by the Saracens. Mortally wounded, he lies down in his armor under a pine tree with his sword beneath him, joins his hands, and expires.[161] If this often-depicted scene—Achille Michallon's well-known painting was reproduced in 1863 in a popular history of art (fig. 33) with which Manet was familiar[162]—does not correspond to the *Orlando muerto* in all respects, it corresponds well enough to explain why it was widely assumed in Manet's time to be the picture's subject.

With the Romantics' interest in the Middle Ages, the *Chanson de Roland* was a subject of renewed scholarly and popular attention, reinforced by the publication of the earliest manuscript of the Old French text in 1837.[163] So it is not surprising that the *Orlando muerto*, which had previously been identified simply as a picture of a dead soldier, is called in the catalogue of a Paris sale in 1827 *The Death of Roland*;[164] nor that it is endowed with an equally impressive provenance in the catalogue of the Pourtalès Collection in 1841: "This beautiful painting, which once decorated one of the palaces of the King of Spain, where it was given the title of *The Dead Roland (Orlando muerto)*."[165] The provenance is just as fanciful as the title and the attribution, since the picture had been in Sweden and Germany before it reached France about 1818, and its author was thought to be a pupil of Van Dyck's rather than Velázquez.[166] Clearly the Pourtalès catalogue, although written by a Louvre curator, was not up to the standard of the Frick's catalogues.

Even if Manet was not as aware of these scholarly publications as you now are, he had surely read the *Chanson de Roland* at school; and even if he had forgotten much of it, he surely remembered the famous episode of Roland's death. Thus an impressive painting, said to represent that subject, and said to be by Velázquez, would have seemed particularly relevant to him in conceiving his *toreador*'s death; and especially if, as I have argued, that death stood for all the deaths at Puebla and elsewhere in Mexico. Just as the ambitious Ganelon betrayed Roland to the Saracen king, so Napoleon III, driven by imperial ambitions, betrayed the French soldiers he had sent to Mexico, and later betrayed Maximilian by withdrawing them.

As for Gérôme's *Dead Caesar*, it could be linked even more easily with Napoleon, and hence with the *Incident in a Bullfight*. The French emperor consciously identified with the Roman emperor and in 1865 published a long biography of him, with a frontispiece commissioned from Gérôme.[167] "Napoléon le Petit," as Victor Hugo called him, promoted himself as a successor to his uncle "Napoléon le Grand," who in turn saw himself as a modern Caesar, and had a statue of himself wearing a Roman toga erected on the Vendôme Column to celebrate his military victories. With the changes of political regime that followed Napoleon's death, the statue was removed; but of course his nephew had a new one erected in 1864.[168] When the Communards, the radicalized populace that controlled Paris at the time, toppled the Vendôme Column in 1871 (fig. 34), the crowd rejoiced that "Caesar was finally laid out on his back"—that the Second Empire itself was finally laid low.[169] So even in 1864 Manet, in using Gérôme's *Dead Caesar* as one of the models for his dead *toreador*, may have alluded to Napoleon as a dictator, just as his image of the slain bullfighter may have alluded to Napoleon and Eugénie's deadly Mexican campaign.

Shortly after the Commune was crushed and Paris was retaken by the conservative government of Adolphe Thiers—the infamous "bloody week" whose aftermath Manet witnessed[170]—he made two lithographs of the street fighting and the executions that swiftly followed. Lithography, unlike etching, was a medium of mass dissemination, and Manet used it several times to make political statements. But more important, in conceiving these prints he recycled images he had already charged with political significance during the Second Empire. The composition of the *Barricade* (fig. 35) repeats in reverse that of the *Execution of the Emperor Maximilian*, and was in turn to have been the basis for a larger picture of the repression of the Commune, never realized but known through a watercolor and gouache study.[171] In transferring the scene to an urban setting, Manet inevitably evokes Goya's *Executions of the Third of May 1808*, the model for all such scenes of annihilation by a firing squad conceived as a pitiless impersonal mechanism, including of course the Maximilian pictures themselves.[172] Of the latter, Manet had also made a lithograph in 1868, hoping he could thereby draw public attention to the event, even if the painted version were to be refused by the Salon. It was indeed refused, as we have seen, but permission to publish the lithograph was also refused.[173] As Zola wrote in excoriating the censors,

> the soldiers shooting Maximilian were wearing a uniform almost identical to that of our own troops. . . . M. Manet, who truly loves truth, has drawn their real costumes, which closely resemble those of the Vincennes infantrymen. . . . An artist has dared to put before their eyes a cruel irony: France shooting Maximilian![174]

In a similar but more barbaric way, France was now shooting Frenchmen. The soldiers shown in the *Barricade* were summarily executing Parisian civilians, without even the court-martial Maximilian had been afforded. In repeating the composition, Manet implies that the tragic consequences of the Parisian conflict are fatally like those of the Mexican conflict, and that Napoleon's reckless policies were ultimately responsible for both.

Similarly, the pose of the dead soldier in the other lithograph of 1871, titled simply *Civil War* (fig. 36), repeats in reverse that of the *Dead Toreador*;[175] just as the stone wall behind him recalls that in the *Execution of the Emperor Maximilian* as a metaphor of callous impersonality.[176] If the fallen bullfighter had stood for the French soldiers killed in Mexico, it could also stand for the soldiers killed in suppressing the Paris Commune. But because once again the uniforms and identities were ambiguous, it could stand as well for the insurgents killed on the other side of the barricades. For a moderate republican like Manet, the extremism of both sides in this civil war was abhorrent. For all his revulsion at the savage suppression of the Commune by "that little twit Thiers," who he hoped would "drop dead in the middle of a speech," he also strongly condemned the Communards as "cowardly assassins," who would "kill off, in the public mind, the sound idea that the only government for honest, peaceful, intelligent people is a republic."[177] The dead on both sides of the barricades were victims of ideological extremes, of ruthless regimes and brutal customs, like the emperor executed at Querétaro, the soldiers slain at Puebla, and the *toreador* gored in Madrid.

*A*fter the traumatic events of 1871, Manet largely avoided treating politically charged subjects on a public scale, though his portrait of Rochefort and scene of Rochefort's escape from the penal colony to which former Communards had been condemned, his portrait of Clemenceau, and his projected portrait of Gambetta show where his political sympathies still lay.[178] When he occasionally treated a tragic subject, it was in a small format and an undramatic manner. In *The Suicide* (fig. 37) of about 1877, the foreshortened figure of the victim recurs, but now sprawled on a bed, a revolver in hand, in a banal urban context that suggests a purely private motive, perhaps financial or sentimental.[179]

This was not the case, however, in the 1860s, when tragic subjects both with and without political content abounded in Manet's work. As we have seen, the *Incident in a Bullfight* became the *Dead Toreador*, no longer a narrative but an emblem of all defeated combatants; and that in turn became the *Dead Man*, a still more universal image of the human condition. But even in its initial state, the *Incident in a Bullfight*, with its stark, looming corpse dominating the composition, was more a meditation on death than a depiction of action and local color. And although the critics seem not to have noticed it, this aspect was reinforced by the picture Manet sent with it to the Salon of 1864, the *Dead Christ with Angels*, a work of comparable size and a similar morbid theme;[180] in effect, the two were conceptual if not physical pendants. A year or two later, he painted two figures brooding about death, one in a religious, the other in a secular mode: the *Monk in Prayer*, a Franciscan friar kneeling in prayer before a skull, and the *Tragic Actor*, a Hamlet-like figure haunted by ghosts and fearful of death.[181] And a year or two after that, he painted *The Execution of the Emperor Maximilian* and *The Burial*, one showing the martyrdom of a prominent leader, the other the funeral of an anonymous citizen, one a monumental figure composition, the other essentially a cityscape, but both revealing Manet's continuing preoccupation with death.[182]

So I want to conclude—yes, finally conclude—by putting aside political allusions and pictorial sources for the *Incident in a Bullfight* and asking instead about feelings, about the artist's emotional investment in his work on a deeper level. I have argued that the picture was begun in the summer or fall of 1862 and inspired by two events: the death of the *matador* Pepete in April and the defeat of the French forces in Mexico in May. Now I would like to add a third event, closer to home: the death of Manet's father in September. Auguste Manet, a senior judge at the Court of First Instance in Paris, had been in poor health for ten years before his death and unable to continue working for the last five, having been stricken with paralysis.[183] Although eventually able to walk again, he never regained his intellectual faculties. This is indeed how he appears in Manet's moving double portrait of his parents (fig. 38) about 1860.[184] How close the two men were, we don't know; but they shared the same upper-middle-class background, the same cultural values, the same political views, and perhaps even the same woman, Suzanne Leenhoff, who may have been the father's mistress before becoming the son's wife. In this scenario, recently elaborated by Nancy Locke, they also "shared" the same son, who was presented to the world as Suzanne's brother Léon Leenhoff, but was biologically Auguste's and in every other way Édouard's.[185] How could the death of a father with whose life his own was so deeply entwined not have found expression in Manet's art, and first of all in the powerful and poignant image of the fallen victim who is still the fallen hero?

*A*s I said at the beginning, if art is long, art history is longer. But it is never long enough, and further questions keep arising. I'm sure that more remains to be said about these deeply felt, richly allusive, and beautifully painted pictures. Or perhaps nothing more should be said, and they should just be looked at. I invite you to leave this room, where you've already been sitting too long, and go into the galleries, where you can see the real thing.

NOTES

I am grateful to several friends at The Frick Collection—to Colin Bailey for inviting me to give the lecture that is published here with minor changes, and to Meredith Watson and Susan Grace Galassi for help with the slides needed to illustrate it; to Elaine Koss for skillfully editing the essay and seeing it through the press, and to Lydia Dufour for timely research in the Library. Ann Hoenigswald of the National Gallery of Art and Dorothy Mahon of The Metropolitan Museum of Art offered their expertise in the technical analysis of the bullfight pictures; and both Álvaro Martínez-Novillo, curator of the Museo de Arte Contemporáneo in Madrid, and Juliet Wilson-Bareau, *doyenne* of independent Manet scholars, generously provided information, documents, and suggestions. As always, I am grateful to my wife, Barbara Divver, for her devoted research assistance and her thoughtful advice and criticism.

Unless otherwise noted, the translations are mine.

1   Lecture on "Manet's *Dead Toreador* and The Frick Collection's *Bullfight*," The Frick Collection, New York, November 20, 1982.

2   Both Jean Rousseau, "Le Salon de 1864," *Le Figaro*, May 12, 1864, pp. 4–5, and Adrien Paul, "Beaux-arts. Salon de 1864," *Le Siècle*, May 29, 1864, p. 1, use this phrase. Jules Claretie, "Le Salon de 1864. Le Salon des Refusés," *L'Artiste*, June 30, 1864, p. 3, adds that the *Incident* was in "la place la meilleure de la salle."

3   Bertall [Charles-Albert d'Arnoux], "Promenade au Salon de 1864," *Le Journal amusant*, May 21, 1864. The caption, "Joujoux espagnols accommodés à la sauce noir de Ribera par M. Manet y Courbetos, y Zurbaran de Las Batignolas," alludes to the influence of Spanish art on both Manet and Courbet.

4   H[enri] Oulevay, "Au Salon de 1864," *Le Monde illustré*, May 28, 1864. The caption, "Un toréador mis en chambre, par Manet," using the idiomatic expression "mettre quelqu'un en chambre" (to dupe someone into losing a game) further explains the domestic setting.

5   Cham [Amédée de Noé], "Une promenade au Salon," *Le Charivari*, May 22, 1864. The caption, "Ayant eu a se plaindre de son marchand de couleurs, M. Manet prend le parti de ne plus se servir que de son encrier," reinforces the point. A fourth caricature, by Paul Hadol, "93 !!! ou les horreurs du Salon de 1864," *La Vie parisienne*, May 28, 1864, pp. 306–8, shows only a bust of a bullfighter; the text refers to "un des Espagnols qui tuent des rats à la lance, de M. Manet."

6   Christopher Parsons and Martha Ward, *A Bibliography of Salon Criticism in Second Empire Paris*, London, 1986, pp. 120–40, the most complete bibliography published thus far of the Salon of 1864, lists 126 reviews. George Heard Hamilton, *Manet and His Critics*, New Haven, 1949, pp. 51–65, excerpts, translates, and analyzes some of the most important ones.

7   The *Incident in a Bullfight* and the *Dead Christ with Angels*, nos. 1282 and 1281, respectively. Catalogued in Denis Rouart and Daniel Wildenstein, *Édouard Manet: catalogue raisonné*, Lausanne, 1975, I, nos. 71 and 74, respectively (cited hereafter as R-W 71, etc.).

8   See Hamilton, *Manet and His Critics*, pp. 43–51.

9   Jules Castagnary, "Salon de 1864," *Le Grand Journal*, June 12, 1864, p. 3. Louis Enault, "L'Exposition des beaux-arts de 1864," *L'Universel*, May 26, 1864, p. 123. Théophile Gautier, "Salon de 1864," *Le Moniteur universel*, June 25, 1864, p. 877. Albert de La Fizelière, "Salon de 1864," *L'Union des arts*, June 25, 1864, p. 1. Jean Rousseau, "Salon de 1864," *L'Univers illustré*, June 15, 1864, p. 379. W. Bürger [Théophile Thoré], "Salon de 1864," *L'Indépendance belge*, June 15, 1864; reprinted in Thoré, *Salons de W. Bürger, 1861–1868*, Paris, 1870, II, pp. 98–99.

10 Paul, "Beaux-arts. Salon de 1864," p. 1. See also Louis Leroy, "Salon de 1864," *Le Charivari*, May 25, 1864: "Le taureau ressemble à une silhouette noire découpée sans le moindre soin."

11 X. Peintre en retraite, "Le Salon de 1864," *Gazette de France*, June 11, 1864, p. 1.

12 Hector de Callias, "Le Salon de 1864," *L'Artiste*, June 1, 1864, p. 242. See also Edmond About, *Salon de 1864*, Paris, 1864, pp. 156–57: "Il aura beau . . . peindre un torero de bois tué par un rat cornu. . . ."

13 E.g., Charles Gueullette, "Salon de 1864. Le Genre," *Les Beaux-arts*, June 1, 1864, p. 327: "On reprochait à M. Manet de peindre avec une brosse à cirage. Son *Épisode d'une course aux taureaux* (no. 1282) est-il moins noir?" See also note 5, above.

14 A.-J. Du Pays, "Salon de 1864," *L'Illustration*, July 16, 1864, p. 38. "See also Henri du Cleuziou, "Flanerie à l'exposition," *Gazette littéraire, artistique et scientifique*, May 28, 1864, p. 55: "[Manet] jette à terre des *Toreadors* noirs sur des fonds jaunes. . . ."

15 Jean Rousseau, "Le Salon de 1864," pp. 4–5: "M. Manet peint l'Espagne comme M. Bonvin peint la France, avec des ombres aussi noirs; seulement ses clairs sont d'un blanc blafard et son rouge brique comme ceux de M. Bonvin."

16 As Éric Darragon points out (*Manet*, Paris, 1991, p. 132), it was mid-twentieth-century American historians, not nineteenth-century French critics, who were troubled by the "abrupt and flattened space of *Mlle V. as an Espada*, where the bull and the *toreadors* are also illogically small in relation to the principal figure" (Hamilton, *Manet and His Critics*,

p. 52), and where as a result "the bull-fighting scene makes an annoying hole in the decorative schema and points up the unreality of this costume-piece" (John Richardson, *Édouard Manet: Paintings and Drawings*, London, 1958, p. 14).

17 See, for example, the *Torero 1er espada*, one of three color lithographs by Achille Devéria after drawings by José Dominguez Becquer, published in *L'Almanach d'Andalousie*, 1836. Manet must have known this print, since he made an oil copy after another one in the same suite in 1862 (R-W 56, where the print is incorrectly identified). For other explanations of, and possible sources for, the distorted perspective, see Manuela B. Mena Marqués, in *Manet en el Prado*, exh. cat., Museo Nacional del Prado, Madrid, 2003, p. 444.

18 Of the writers who state that he was reacting to the criticism, the only early source is Edmond Bazire; the others are later art historians. See the publications listed by Charles S. Moffett in *Manet, 1832–1883*, exh. cat., Galeries Nationales du Grand Palais, Paris, 1983, p. 198, n. 4, and Bazire, *Manet*, Paris, 1884, p. 42.

19 Antonin Proust, *Édouard Manet, souvenirs*, ed. A. Barthélemy, Paris, 1913, p. 47. This passage, which does not occur in the first version of Proust's text, published in *La Revue blanche*, February-May 1897, p. 173, was added by his former secretary Barthélemy on the basis of Proust's unpublished notes.

20 Although the original tacking margins, wrapped around the stretcher, were removed at an unknown date when the painting was relined, the present edges presumably followed the original ones closely; see Ann Hoenigswald, "Technical Observations," in Susan Grace Galassi et al., *Manet's* The Dead Toreador *and* The Bullfight, New York, 1999, p. 21, n. 2.

21 Martel Caristie, "Le Salon de 1864," *Revue du monde colonial*, June 1864, p. 509: "*L'Épisode du combat de taureaux* est digne d'être mis en pièces et enfermé dans l'une de ces boîtes à joujoux qu'on donne pour étrennes aux enfants terribles."

22 Moffett in *Manet, 1832–1883*, p. 114.

23 Jules Castagnary, "Salon de 1864," *Le Grand Journal*, June 12, 1864, p. 3.

24 Michael Fried, *Manet's Modernism: or, The Face of Painting in the 1860s*, Chicago, 1996, pp. 267–80.

25 In a conversation reported by Mallarmé. See Philippe Verdier, "Stéphane Mallarmé: 'Les Impressionnistes et Édouard Manet,' 1875–1876," *Gazette des beaux-arts*, November 1975, p. 149. Zola, too, remarked: "En commençant un tableau, jamais il n'aurait pu dire comment ce tableau viendrait." Émile Zola, "Préface," *Exposition des oeuvres d'Éd. Manet*, Paris, 1884; in his *Écrits sur l'art*, ed. Jean-Pierre Leduc-Adine, Paris, 1991, p. 454.

26 R-W 52 and 53, respectively. For comprehensive information on the provenance, exhibition history, and bibliography of each work, see the National Gallery of Art's Web

site (www.nga.gov) and *The Frick Collection: An Illustrated Catalogue*, II, ed. Bernice David-son, Princeton, 1968, pp. 152–56.

27 Cited in note 62, below.

28 *The Fifer* is R-W 113. Other examples are *The Tragic Actor* and *The Matador Saluting*, R-W 106 and 111, respectively. All three emulate the effect Manet had admired in Velázquez's *Portrait of Pablillos de Valladolid* in the Prado: "Le fond disparaît, c'est de l'air qui entoure ce bonhomme tout habillé de noir et vivant." Letter to Henri Fantin-Latour, September 3, 1865, in *Édouard Manet: voyage en Espagne*, ed. Juliet Wilson-Bareau, Caen, 1988, p. 44.

29 Letter to Louis Martinet, director of the Société, datable to February 15–17, 1865; see Juliet Wilson-Bareau, *Manet by Himself*, Boston, 1991, p. 32. Of the eight pictures he list-ed, Manet sent only six and showed only two, and those for only a day or two, before resigning from the Société; see Hippolyte Lejosne's letter to Baudelaire, February 21, 1865, cited in Sophie Monneret, *L'Impressionnisme et son époque*, Paris, 1987, I, p. 505. Whether the *Dead Toreador* was one of them, as some writers have stated, is not known.

30 Charles Pérussaux, "Manet coupeur de toiles," *Les Lettres françaises*, September 15, 1955. See also Anne Coffin Hanson, "Édouard Manet, 'Les Gitanos,' and the Cut Canvas," *The Burlington Magazine*, March 1970, pp. 158–66.

31 See Ernest Fillonneau, "Cercle de l'union artistique. Exposition annuelle," *Le Moniteur des arts*, March 27, 1866; cited in Darragon, *Manet*, p. 140. Fillonneau remarks on Manet's unexpected presence in this conservative venue.

32 *Catalogue des tableaux de M. Édouard Manet exposés avenue de l'Alma en 1867*, Paris, 1867, no. 5: *L'Homme mort*. The picture was shown again with this title at the Exposition Maritime Internationale du Havre in June–September 1868; see Moffett in *Manet, 1832–1883*, p. 195. Its presence there can probably be explained by the bullfights that were held at Le Havre to draw crowds to the Exposition; see Charles Yriarte, "Courrier de Paris," *Le Monde illustré*, May 30, 1868, pp. 338–39.

33 Jean C. Harris, *Édouard Manet: Graphic Works; A Definitive Catalogue Raisonné*, New York, 1970, no. 55; third state (cited hereafter as H 55, etc.). In the print, the ground and background are more clearly separated than in the painting. The same is true of the earliest photographs of the *Dead Toreador*—the one taken by Fernand Lochard in 1872 (Paris, Bibliothèque Nationale de France, Cabinet des Estampes, Dépôt Légal, no. 872.22) and the one taken for Charles Durand-Ruel, presumably in 1872 or 1892, when he owned the picture (reproduced in Louis Hourticq, Jean Laran, and Georges Le Bas, *Manet*, Paris, n.d. [1911], opp. p. 36). The photographs also reveal more varied brushstrokes in the background and more details of the *toreador*'s costume than are vis-

ible today, which suggests a gradual alteration of the colors or retouching by a later hand.

34 Theodore Reff, *Manet and Modern Paris*, Chicago, 1982, pp. 214–15. Ann Hoenigswald and Sarah Fisher, of the Conservation Division of the National Gallery of Art, were of invaluable help in reading and interpreting the x-radiographs. Such a reconstruction had already been attempted by Julius Meier-Graefe eighty years earlier, but without success; see his *Édouard Manet*, Munich, 1912, p. 66, n. 1.

35 See Susan Galassi's essay in Galassi et al., *Manet's* The Dead Toreador *and* The Bullfight, pp. 7–18, and Hoenigswald, "Technical Observations," pp. 19–21. In "Another View of Manet's Bullfight Pictures," ibid., pp. 22–24, Malcolm Park and Juliet Wilson-Bareau argue that "Manet added the large, foreground figure of the dead *toreador* or *matador* after completing the composition" of the first version, since "the scales of the dead *toreador* and the bull are incongruous, and so too is the relative size of the distant *toreros*." It seems unlikely, however, that Manet would have used so large a canvas for so anecdotal a subject as that shown in their fig. 8, which lacks the monumental scale and dramatic impact of a picture intended for the Salon. And as we have already seen, there are other ways to explain such discrepancies in scale, which moreover had already been present in earlier pictures such as *Mlle V . . . in the Costume of an Espada*.

36 Charles Asselineau, "Salon de 1864," *Revue nationale et étrangère*, June 10, 1864, pp. 286–87.

37 Galassi et al., *Manet's* The Dead Toreador *and* The Bullfight, p. 19 and pl. 4.

38 This is also the opinion of Park and Wilson-Bareau, in ibid., p. 22 and fig. 8.

39 Ibid., p. 19 and pl. 5.

40 Still unanswered is the question of the size of the *Incident in a Bullfight*. To judge from the composite photographs in Galassi's and Hoenigswald's essays (ibid., pls. 3–5) and the diagrams in Park and Wilson-Bareau's essay (ibid., figs. 8–9), it must have been about 128 x 166 cm. This is also the size, to within a centimeter, of *Mlle V . . . in the Costume of an Espada*, the only other bullfight picture Manet painted before going to Spain; and this confirms my belief that the *Incident*, too, should be dated to 1862. For both pictures, he may have used a standard *100 Figure* stretcher of 162 x 130 cm. With the cutting up of the one and the relining of the other, neither of the original stretchers survives.

41 Charles Limet, *Un Vétéran du barreau parisien, quatre-vingts ans de souvenirs (1827–1907)*, Paris, 1908, p. 249: "J'étais depuis longtemps (depuis le coup d'état) un habitué de la maison." Limet (1820–after 1914), who was known in his later years as "le doyen des avocats parisiens," also published many volumes of poetry.

42 Ibid., p. 205.

43 Limet had gone on a walking tour from Strasbourg to Venice with the lawyer and future liberal politician Émile Ollivier, who was to become a good friend of Manet's. See Ollivier's *Journal*, ed. Theodore Zeldin and Anne Troisier de Diaz, Paris, 1961, I, p. 16; and Marie-Thérèse Ollivier, *Émile Ollivier, sa jeunesse, d'après son journal et sa correspondance*, Paris, 1919, pp. 225–29.

44 Jacques de Biez, *Édouard Manet: conférence faite à la salle des Capucines, le mardi 22 janvier 1884*, Paris, 1884, p. 33, mentions such a trip along with those to Italy and Holland in the early 1850s. Proust, in "Édouard Manet, souvenirs," p. 169, implies that it took place in 1852, shortly after Manet admired a bullfight picture at the Salon of 1851.

45 Neither Bazire, *Manet*, pp. 10–12, who discusses Manet's trips to several other countries, nor Théodore Duret, *Histoire d'Édouard Manet et de son oeuvre*, Paris, 1919 [1st ed. 1902], p. 46, who recounts his sojourn in Madrid with Manet in 1865, mentions such a trip in 1852. Nor is one noted in any of the more recent literature on the artist.

46 From a notice in *Le Journal de Paris*, April 14, 1781, quoted in Georges Bertin, "Les Combats de taureaux à Paris," *Revue de la Révolution*, February 1887, p. 162. On the Combat du Taureau, see Dr. Ph[ilippe] Dally, *Belleville, histoire d'une localité parisienne pendant la Révolution*, Paris, 1912, pp. 73–76.

47 Bertin, "Les Combats de taureaux," p. 167, gives the date as 1833. But Dally, *Belleville*, p. 75, shows that it was after 1840. And Jacques Hillairet, *Dictionnaire historique des rues de Paris*, Paris, 1963, I, p. 371, says it was shortly before 1850.

48 Passed on July 2, 1850, the law was sponsored by Jacques Philippe Delmas de Grammont (1796–1862), a député de la Loire who was president of the Société Protectrice des Animaux and general of a cavalry division. See Pierre Larousse, *Grand dictionnaire universel du xixe siècle*, Paris, 1866–90, I, p. 390. Larousse himself was an ardent supporter of the legislation and of the liberal, republican values it represented.

49 On the ideological conflict, to which I shall return, see Maurice Agulhon, "Le Sang des bêtes: le problème de la protection des animaux en France au xixe siècle," in Agulhon, *Histoire vagabonde*, Paris, 1988, I, esp. pp. 261–82.

50 Robert Fernier, *La Vie et l'oeuvre de Gustave Courbet: catalogue raisonné*, Lausanne, 1977, I, no. 157. Fernier dates it to 1854–56, with no explanation, and cites Courbet's letter to Amand Gautier of July 1858 mentioning "cette esquisse de l'hippodrome où il y a une course de taureau." A terminus is provided by the destruction in July 1856 of the Hippodrome, which is shown in the background; see Hillairet, *Dictionnaire historique des rues de Paris*, II, pp. 296 and 633. According to Jean-Jacques Fernier, private correspondence, the picture was in the collection of François Bel, Paris, in 1983.

51 See the engraving of the Hippodrome in Edmond Texier, *Tableau de Paris*, I, Paris, 1852, p. 4.

52 Théophile Gautier, "Hippodrome—course de taureaux," *La Presse*, August 20, 1849, pp. 1–2.

53 "Nouvelles diverses," *Le Monde dramatique*, October 9, 1862, p. 4: "On annonce qu'une compagnie de torréadors [*sic*] vient d'obtenir l'autorisation de donner à l'Hippodrome de véritables combats de taureaux, comme à Madrid." A similar project, also unrealized, was reported in *Le Chroniqueur de la semaine*, October 6, 1856, p. 28: "On annonce qu'une compagnie industrielle a déposé aujourd'hui, à la préfecture de police, une autorisation de construire un cirque pour les courses de taureaux. Cette autorisation, déjà sollicitée sous plusieurs gouvernements, a toujours été accueillie par un même refus."

54 The Flor di Sevilla troupe was listed in the daily *Figaro-programme* as performing from August 12 through October 8. For Manet's painting *The Spanish Ballet* (R-W 55) and related portraits of Lola de Valence and Mariano Camprubi (ibid., nos. 53 and 54), all made at this time, see Françoise Cachin in *Manet, 1832–1883*, pp. 144–50.

55 R-W 110; dated there to 1866, it is more likely that it was conceived as a counterpart to *The Spanish Ballet* and therefore also painted in 1862. The two pictures show the same table and bench and the same background figures, based on Goya's *Art of Bullfighting*; see note 56, below.

56 For Blanchard's *Toreros avant la course*, a large colored lithograph published by Goupil in 1852, see Paul Guinard, *Dauzats et Blanchard, peintres de l'Espagne romantique*, Paris, 1967, pp. 392–93, no. 70, and pl. xlv. On the other sources cited, see Joel Isaacson, in *Manet and Spain, Prints and Drawings*, exh. cat., Museum of Art, University of Michigan, Ann Arbor, 1969, pp. 33–34.

57 Initially, only five performances were planned from August 26 through September 3; see the *Gazette des étrangers*, August 19, 1865, p. 2. But despite the strict limitations, the event proved so popular that thousands of people had to be turned away; see *Figaro-programme*, August 30, 1865, p. 2. Additional performances were then arranged through September 18; see *Le Foyer dramatique*, September 16–18, 1865, p. 2.

58 See the mocking reviews in *Le Monde illustré*, August 26, 1865, p. 131, and in *L'Univers illustré*, September 6, 1865, p. 562.

59 Letter from Astruc to Manet, about August 22, 1865, in *Édouard Manet: voyage en Espagne*, pp. 29–40, esp. pp. 34 and 38. An enthusiastic Hispanophile, Astruc prepared an elaborate itinerary, much of which Manet ignored.

60 Letter to Charles Baudelaire, September 14, 1865, in ibid., p. 48.

61 Letter to Zacharie Astruc, September 17, 1865, in ibid., p. 50.

62 These are, respectively, R-W 107 and 108. See also R-W 109, painted at about the

same time. As for the watercolor Manet purportedly made in Madrid (see Nicholas Turner, *J. Paul Getty Museum: European Drawings*, IV, Los Angeles, 2000, pp. 232–34), Juliet Wilson-Bareau has rightly questioned its authenticity: "Manet and Spain," in *Manet / Velázquez: The French Taste for Spanish Painting*, exh. cat., The Metropolitan Museum of Art, New York, 2003, p. 239, n. 101.

63   Proust, "Édouard Manet, souvenirs," p. 169. Gabriel Séailles, *Alfred Dehodencq, l'homme et l'artiste*, Paris, 1910, pp. 41–46. The picture entered the Musée du Luxembourg before 1852, was transferred to the Louvre in 1883, and to the Musée de Pau in 1886; see *Le Musée du Luxembourg en 1874*, exh. cat., Grand Palais, Paris, 1974, no. 64.

64   Edmond Dehodencq's etching is illustrated in Séailles, *Alfred Dehodencq*, opp. p. 27. On the vogue of painted and printed bullfight scenes, see Paul Guinard, "Romantiques français en Espagne," *Art de France*, II, 1962, pp. 179–98. For Manet's painted copy of such a print, see note 17, above.

65   Guinard, *Dauzats et Blanchard*, pp. 392–94. Blanchard had previously executed fifteen drawings to illustrate Baron Isidore Taylor's *Voyage pittoresque en Espagne* in 1832, ibid., pp. 388–91, and fifteen watercolors on tauromachian subjects for Count Anatole Demidoff in 1835, ibid., pp. 385–88.

66   Gustave Doré and Charles Davillier, "Voyage en Espagne. Valence—combat de taureaux," *Le Tour du monde*, VI, part 2, 1862, pp. 337–52. This was the third installment in a series that began in 1862, continued almost annually until 1868, and was then published as *L'Espagne*, Paris, 1874. See *Gustave Doré*, exh. cat., Cabinet des Estampes, Musée d'Art Moderne, Strasbourg, 1983, p. 310, no. 652.

67   In the following decades, those of Impressionism, the striking black tones were seen as an aesthetic rather than a dramatic quality. Armand Silvestre called the picture "la plus complète symphonie en noir majeur qui ait été jamais tentée"; "L'École de peinture contemporaine," *La Renaissance littéraire et artistique*, September 28, 1872, p. 179. And Joséphin Péladan praised "les beaux noirs dont on a fait mérite à Manet"; "Le Procédé de Manet d'après l'Exposition faite à l'École des Beaux-Arts," *L'Artiste*, February 1884, p. 109.

68   Both were by Spanish artists and were shown at the Salon of 1855 in connection with the Exposition Universelle: no. 562, Manuel Castellano, *Chevaux tués dans une course de taureaux*; and no. 591, Eugenio Lucas, *Combats de taureaux, à Madrid*. The idea that Lucas knew and even collaborated with Manet is rightly treated with skepticism by Álvaro Martínez-Novillo, *Le Peintre et la tauromachie*, trans. Louis Audibert, Paris, 1988, p. 90.

69   Philippe-Auguste Jourde (1816–1905), formerly a judge in the Tribunal de Commerce, was the managing director of *Le Siècle*, a republican newspaper opposed to

Napoléon III. Jourde was also a collector of Realist and Impressionist art and a friend of Théodore Duret's and Eva Gonzalès's. A letter from him to Manet, dated 1875, is known: Paris, Bibliothèque de l'Institut national d'histoire de l'art, collections Jacques Doucet, carton 59, dossier 3, lettre 24.

70 *Le Siècle*, April 30, 1862, p. 1. Not surprisingly, the article was reprinted in the *Bulletin de la société protectrice des animaux*, IX, 1863, p. 106, along with other recent accounts of fatal injuries in French and Spanish bullrings.

71 According to Hans Tietze, "Manet and a So-Called Velázquez," *The Burlington Magazine*, August 1936, p. 85, "one of the Spaniards of Lola de Valence's troupe was the model for the figure of the *toreador*." Tietze refers only to Manet's "biographers" as his source, but none of them mentions this fact. He may have been recalling Duret's statement (*Histoire d'Édouard Manet et de son oeuvre*, p. 20), itself incorrect, about Manet's *Spanish Singer*: "Le chanteur avait été pris dans cette troupe de musiciens et de danseurs qui lui fournissait aussi le *Ballet espagnol* et *Lola de Valence*. Il avait donc le mérite d'être un véritable Espagnol."

72 On the career of José Rodríguez, known as Pepete (1824–1862), see José María de Cossío, *Los Toros: tratado técnico e histórico*, Madrid, 1943, III, pp. 801–4. The portrait photograph illustrated here is reproduced from p. 802; another is on p. 803.

73 See de Cossío, *Los Toros*, III, p. 804; and Natalio Rivas, *Toreros del romanticismo: anecdotario taurino*, Madrid, 1987, pp. 217–28.

74 The anonymous wash drawing is reproduced from Lorenzo Ortiz-Cañavate, "El Torero español," in *Folklore y costumbres de España*, ed. F. Carreras y Candi, Barcelona, 1931, I, p. 512, where unfortunately no information on its author or date is given.

75 *Catalogo de la fotografías que se venden en casa de J. Laurent, fotógrafo*, Madrid, 1863, nos. 362–64. These three photographs and one of the bull who killed Pepete were already advertised on April 21, 1862; see *Exposición del Antiguo Madrid*, Sociedad Española de Amigos de Arte, 1926, p. 336, no. 38. On Laurent's activities, see *La Fotografía en España hasta 1900*, exh. cat., Biblioteca Nacional, Madrid, 1982, pp. 56–60.

76 See Atsushi Miura, "La Vision photographique dans *Combat de taureaux* de Manet," *Revue de l'art*, no. 79, 1988, pp. 73–75.

77 See R-W 76; and Juliet Wilson-Bareau and David C. Degener, *Manet and the American Civil War: The Battle of U.S.S.* Kearsarge *and C.S.S.* Alabama, New Haven, 2003, p. 15.

78 R-W 124–27; H 54. See Nils Gösta Sandblad, *Manet, Three Studies in Artistic Conception*, trans. Walter Nash, Lund, 1954, pp. 199–261; and Juliet Wilson-Bareau, "Manet and the Execution of Maximilian," in Wilson-Bareau et al., *Manet: The Execution of Maximilian; Painting, Politics, and Censorship*, London, 1992, pp. 48–62.

79   See de Cossio, *Los Toros*, III, p. 804.

80   *The Art of Bullfighting*, No. 33: *The Unlucky Death of Pepe Illo in the Ring at Madrid*. The event, probably witnessed by Goya, had occurred on May 11, 1801; and the etchings were published in 1816 and again in 1855; see Enrique Lafuente Ferrari, *Francisco Goya y Lucientes, la Tauromaquia*, trans. Mathilde Pomès, Paris, 1963, pp. 139–45.

81   Henry Fouquier, "Salon de 1864," *Le Peuple*, May 26, 1864, p. 3.

82   Gautier, "Salon de 1864," p. 877.

83   See, for example, Rousseau, "Le Salon de 1864" (*Figaro* version), pp. 4–5; Peintre en retraite, "Le Salon de 1864," p. 1; and especially Bürger (Thoré), "Salon de 1864," pp. 98–99. Thoré had already linked Manet and Goya in reviewing the Salon des Refusés in 1863; *Salons de W. Bürger*, I, p. 424.

84   See Nigel Glendinning, "A New View of Goya's *Tauromaquia*," *Journal of the Warburg and Courtauld Institutes*, XXIV, 1961, pp. 124–25; and Janis A. Tomlinson, *Goya in the Twilight of Enlightenment*, New Haven, 1992, p. 175.

85   See Richard Holt, *Sport and Society in Modern France*, Hamden, Conn., 1981, pp. 104–8; and Agulhon, "Le Sang des bêtes," pp. 273–82.

86   Dr. [Henri] Blatin, *Les Courses de taureaux*, Paris, 1863, pp. 22–28. Published on May 5, according to the *Journal général de l'imprimerie et de la librairie*, 1863, part 1, p. 214, this text had first appeared in the *Bulletin de la société protectrice des animaux*, IX, 1863, pp. 90–123.

87   See Agulhon, "Le Sang des bêtes," p. 263. In identifying Henri Blatin (1806–1869) as a "député de gauche sous la IIIe République," Agulhon confuses him with his brother Antoine Blatin (1841–1911), though they may well have held the same political convictions. On both men, see *Dictionnaire de biographie française*, ed. J. Balteau et al., Paris, 1933–, VI, col. 651.

88   See notes 63 and 68, above.

89   On the moralist and philosopher Ernest Bersot (1816–1880), a scholar of the French Enlightenment and Director of the École normale supérieure, see the biographical notice by Edmond Scherer in Ernest Bersot, *Un Moraliste. Études et pensées d'Ernest Bersot*, Paris, 1882.

90   Ibid, pp. 268–70; cited in Agulhon, "Le Sang des bêtes," pp. 279–80. Conflicting views on bullfighting existed even in the radical left; see the exchange of unsigned articles in *Le Révolté: organe communiste-anarchiste*, January 8, 1887, pp. 3–4, and January 22, 1887, pp. 1–2.

91   Limet, *Un Vétéran du barreau parisien*, pp. 188–90.

92   Proust, "Édouard Manet, souvenirs," pp. 130–31. See also the moving account in Bazire, *Manet*, pp. 6–9.

93 Édouard Manet, *Lettres de jeunesse 1848–1849, voyage à Rio*, Paris, 1928, p. 67. See also his let-ter to his cousin Jules Dejouy, ibid., p. 60.

94 On Manet's political convictions, see Philip Nord, "Manet and Radical Politics," *Jour-nal of Interdisciplinary History*, Winter 1989, pp. 447–80. For his portraits of Rochefort and other radical republican politicians, see note 178, below.

95 Harris 80. On its political content, see Reff, *Manet and Modern Paris*, p. 124. Marilyn Brown's rejection of this interpretation, in "Manet, Nodier, and Polichinelle," *Art Jour-nal*, Spring 1985, pp. 43–48, makes too little of the statements of Lemercier's assistant and of Edmond Bazire that I cited, and in citing Nodier's conception of Polichinelle in 1830, ignores the more relevant conception of him in 1874, that of an "homme sans consistance, sans fixité dans le caractère" (Larousse, *Grand dictionnaire universel du xixe siècle*, XII, p. 1296).

96 See Agulhon, "Le Sang des bêtes," p. 262.

97 Gautier, "Hippodrome—course de taureaux," p. 1. See also Théophile Gautier, *Voyage en Espagne*, Paris, 1859 [1st ed. 1845], p. 72: "Une course de taureaux est un des plus beaux spectacles que l'homme puisse imaginer."

98 Victor Hugo, speaking in support of passage of the Loi Grammont; cited in Christian Meynard, "La Véritable histoire de la corrida" (www.spa-de-quevaucamps.com/corri-da.htm). I have not found this passage in the more likely places in Hugo's vast writings.

99 *Le Siècle*, April 30, 1862, p. 1.

100 See Auguste Lafront, *Histoire de la corrida en France du Second Empire à nos jours*, Paris, 1977, pp. 9–22. *The Times* (London), October 1, 1852, p. 3, noted that "no difficulties were encountered on the part of the local authorities; on the contrary, every encouragement was given. . . ."

101 See Lafront, *Histoire de la corrida en France*, pp. 23–33; and the account of the ceremonies in *The Times* (London), September 18, 1856, p. 10.

102 See Jasper Ridley, *Napoleon III and Eugénie*, London, 1979, pp. 160–62.

103 *Les Femmes galantes des Napoléons, secrets de cour et palais, documents et conversations authentiques*, Parts IV, V, VI, London, 1862, pp. 161–64. The anonymous author, in fact Eugène de Mirecourt [pseud. of Charles Jacquot], was notorious for his calumnious biographies of contemporaries.

104 That Goya's *Art of Bullfighting*, No. 5, was a model for the bullfight, and that Nos. 16, 19, and 28 were models for the men standing near the barrier and for the figure climbing over it, has long been recognized; see Isaacson, in *Manet and Spain, Prints and Drawings*, p. 31.

105 See Moffett in *Manet, 1832–1883*, p. 114.

106 It appears to be the same costume, without the white cummerbund, that the *Young Man in the Costume of a Mayo* (R-W 70) wears, and that Marqués, in *Manet en el Prado*, p. 445, describes as "a Maragato muleteer's costume with European dandyish details."

107 R-W 54. For the costume prints, see note 17, above; for the travel books, Gautier, *Voyage en Espagne*, pp. 76–78, and Alexandre Dumas, *Impressions de voyage. De París à Cadix*, Paris, 1880 (1st ed. 1847), I, pp. 101 and 112.

108 See Marqués, in *Manet en el Prado*, p. 443.

109 *Les Femmes galantes des Napoléons*, pp. 226–27.

110 The artist, François, prince de Joinville (1818–1900), was presumably a member of her circle; see Jean-Marie Moulin, *Guide du musée national du château de Compiègne*, Paris, 1992, p. 140 and fig. 23.

111 See Elizabeth Anne McCauley, *A.A.E. Disdéri and the Carte de Visite Portrait Photograph*, New Haven, 1985, pp. 181–87; A photograph of a *torera* attributed to Laurent is illustrated in Lee Fontanella, *La Historia de la fotografía en España*, Madrid, 1981, p. 185.

112 See Cossío, *Los Toros*, I, pp. 747–57. Illustrated in ibid., p. 751, is Doré's engraving (dated elsewhere to 1867) of the Andalusian *matador* Teresa Bolsi, which he obviously copied from the photograph of her illustrated in ibid., p. 750.

113 Manet may also have had a private source of gossip about the empress, since a fellow student in Thomas Couture's studio, Count de Lezay-Marnézia, became one of her chamberlains in 1861, while retaining his interest in contemporary art; see Proust, "Édouard Manet, souvenirs," p. 172.

114 See Nancy Nichols Barker, *Distaff Diplomacy; The Empress Eugénie and the Foreign Policy of the Second Empire*, Austin, 1967, p. 87 and n. 21.

115 See Ridley, *Napoleon III and Eugénie*, p. 498, and Douglas Johnson, "The French Intervention in Mexico: A Historical Background," in *Manet: The Execution of Maximilian*, pp. 18–21.

116 Barker, *Distaff Diplomacy*, pp. 92–93. On José Manuel Hidalgo y Esnaurrizar (1828–1896), a friend of Eugénie's from her girlhood in Madrid and now her closest adviser, see ibid., pp. 88–89, and Ridley, *Napoleon III and Eugénie*, pp. 499 and 511.

117 See note 78, above.

118 See Sandblad, *Manet*, p. 146; Isaacson, in *Manet and Spain, Prints and Drawings*, p. 38; and George L. Mauner, *Manet, Peintre-Philosophe: A Study of the Painter's Themes*, University Park, Penn., 1975, p. 123.

119 See Larousse, *Grand dictionnaire universel du xixe siècle*, IV, p. 378.

120 According to Cossío, *Los Toros*, IV, p. 149, the suppression began immediately. According to the *Enciclopedia de México*, ed. José Álvarez, Mexico City, 1988, XIII, p. 7772, it

began in 1873 and continued to 1886. On the promotion of bullfighting during Maximilian's reign, see Colonel Ch[arles] Blanchot, *L'Intervention française au Méxique*, Paris, 1911, II, pp. 184–85.

121 See especially *The Art of Bullfighting*, Nos. 13, 20, 26, and 30. As Marqués notes, in *Manet en el Prado*, p. 469, "The strange figure of the woman at the top of the group [in the Mannheim version], wearing a mantilla and a carnation in her hair, hiding her face behind a fan, resembles one of the *Majas* from Goya's *Caprichos*, and in her graceful serenity she looks as if she is in the bullring, waiting for the bullfighter to dedicate the bull to her before killing it." Is she then an allusion to the Empress Eugénie, with her twin passions of Spanish bullfighting and Mexican intervention?

122 Janis A. Tomlinson, "Goya's *Tauromaquia*: The Bullfight as Political Allegory," unpublished paper delivered at the 71st annual meeting of the College Art Association, Philadelphia, February 17–19, 1983.

123 See Jules Claretie, *Journées de voyage. Espagne et France*, Paris, 1870, p. 252, describing the *matador* El Tato performing: "Il est de noir vêtu, et les ornements de sa veste sont de jais. Il porte le deuil de Cucharès, son beau-père. . . ."

124 See Gustave Léon Niox, *Expédition du Mexique, 1861–1867, récit politique et militaire*, Paris, 1874, p. 167; and *Histoire militaire de la France*, ed. Jean Delmas, Paris, 1992, II, p. 522.

125 See Frank Edward Lally, *French Opposition to the Mexican Policy of the Second Empire*, Baltimore, 1931, pp. 32, 41, and 76–85; and Lynn M. Case, *French Opinion on the United States and Mexico, 1860–1867*, New York, 1936, pp. 310–12.

126 Adolphe Tabarant, *Manet et ses oeuvres*, Paris, 1947, pp. 75 and 80. Tabarant got much of his information from Suzanne Manet and Léon Leenhoff about 1900. Yet in *Manet, histoire catalographique*, Paris, 1931, pp. 119–22, he states with equal confidence that Manet painted the *Incident* "from October 1863 to March 1864," shortly before sending it to the Salon.

127 See his letter to the Surintendant des Beaux-Arts, late February 1864, requesting an eight- to ten-day extension, which was denied; Paris, Archives des Musées nationaux, Salon de 1864, Correspondance (artistes), fol. 59. He needed the extension not for the *Incident in a Bullfight* but for the picture he planned to submit with it. By late March, with the *Dead Christ with Angels* evidently still unfinished, the two pictures he had chosen were "les *Courses de Chantilly* et la *Mort du Torreador* [*sic*]," according to the "Bruits du Salon" in *L'Union des arts*, April 2, 1864, p. 3. The racetrack picture, which would have been a thematic pendant to the bullfight picture, was presumably the *View of a Race in the Bois de Boulogne*, which Manet also subsequently cut up; see Jean C. Harris, "Manet's Racetrack Paintings," *The Art Bulletin*, March 1966, pp. 78–82, and Reff, *Manet and Modern Paris*, pp. 132–35.

128 See Wilson-Bareau, "Manet and the Execution of Maximilian," pp. 38–40.

129 Thus, the *Capture of the Fort of San Xavier, near Puebla, March 29, 1863*, was shown at the Salon of 1867 (Wilson-Bareau et al., *Manet: The Execution of Maximilian*, p. 39); *General Forey Leading the French Expeditionary Force into Mexico City* at the Salon of 1868 (ibid., p. 24); and the *Combat at Camarón (Mexico), 30 April 1863*, at the Salon of 1869 (ibid., p. 22).

130 Nordley, "Salon militaire. Lettres sur l'exposition de 1864," *Revue militaire*, May 20, 1864, p. 92.

131 Salon de 1864, no. 977: Ange-Louis Janet-Lange, *Combat d'Altesco, 14 avril; épisode de la guerre du Mexique*. See Alphonse Audéoud, "Exposition de 1864," *Revue indépendante*, July 1, 1864, p. 763, and the wood engraving in *L'Illustration*, May 21, 1864, p. 328, which transforms the event into a traditional equestrian battle.

132 Wilson-Bareau, "Manet and the Execution of Maximilian," pp. 43–44. My own interpretation, although developed independently since 1983, is now indebted in many respects to Wilson-Bareau's.

133 See note 9, above; and on Thoré's career, Frances Suzman Jowell, "Vermeer and Thoré-Bürger: Recoveries of Reputation," *Studies in the History of Art*, LV, 1998, pp. 35–58.

134 Nor does Eugène Spuller, a leftist politician and writer who would also have been alert to the political implications of the *Incident in a Bullfight*. He is clearly thinking of that picture when he describes *l'Homme mort* in Manet's 1867 exhibition as "étendu sur le sable de l'arène des combats de taureaux," but he comments only on its "netteté rigoureuse" and "science consommée"; "Édouard Manet et sa peinture," *Le Nain jaune*, June 8, 1867, p. 5.

135 Désiré François Laugée (1823–1896), a pupil of Picot's, was a painter of history, portraits, and genre. His picture (Salon de 1864, no. 1116), which treated a subject of great current interest, was both a critical and a popular success.

136 See Lally, *French Opposition to the Mexican Policy of the Second Empire*, pp. 63–64 and 70–73.

137 See especially the descriptions by Édouard Lockroy, "Salon de 1864," *L'Esprit public*, June 5, 1864, p. 1, and by Achille de Lauzières-Thémines, "Salon de 1864," *La Patrie*, June 11, 1864, p. 3.

138 See the anonymous report in *La Chronique des arts et de la curiosité*, February 7, 1869, in "Documents Relating to the 'Maximilian Affair,'" ed. Juliet Wilson-Bareau, in *Manet, 1832–1883*, p. 532.

139 John House, "Manet's Maximilian: History Painting, Censorship, and Ambiguity," in *Manet: The Execution of Maximilian*, p. 100.

140 See the catalogue entry by Javier Portús Pérez, in *Manet / Velázquez*, p. 459.

141 See Marqués, in *Manet en el Prado*, p. 455. But Marqués's notion that the dead *toreador* lacks any "transcendent human dignity" because, unlike the dead soldier, it is "bereft of any religious references" would probably have been alien to Manet.

142 See Hanson, "Édouard Manet, 'Les Gitanos,' and the Cut Canvas," p. 161.

143 Gautier, "Salon de 1864," p. 877.

144 Bürger (Thoré), "Salon de 1864," p. 98. Manet's reliance on the Velázquez was noted twice, independently of Thoré—by Fillonneau, "Cercle de l'union artistique," p. 2, and by Péladan, "Le Procédé de Manet," p. 109.

145 Undated letter, datable to c. June 15, 1864; Charles Baudelaire, *Lettres, 1841–1866*, Paris, 1906, p. 362; as translated in Hamilton, *Manet and His Critics*, pp. 62–63.

146 Bürger (Thoré), "Salon de 1864," *L'Indépendance belge*, June 26, 1864; reprinted in Thoré, *Salons de W. Bürger*, II, pp. 137–38.

147 Adolphe Joanne, *Paris illustré, nouveau guide de l'étranger et du Parisien*, Paris, 1863, pp. 701–2; cited in Wilson-Bareau, "Manet and Spain," p. 230, n. 71. Darragon, *Manet*, p. 141, notes a watercolor copy of the *Orlando* shown at the Salon of 1864 (no. 2374), which must have been made in the gallery itself, since the picture had not been reproduced in color.

148 The photographs included in *Souvenirs de la galerie Pourtalès. Tableaux anciens et objets d'art; photographiés par Goupil et Cie.*, Paris, 1863, were first published in fascicles of twelve, beginning in October 1862; see *Les Albums de Napoléon III*, ed. Sylvie Aubenas, Paris, 2004, p. 166, n. 4, and *La Chronique des arts et de la curiosité*, February 8, 1863, p. 120. If they appeared in the same order as the plates in the final album, then the fourth fascicle, containing the "Orlando muerto" (pl. 38), would have appeared in January 1863.

149 Gerald Ackerman, *Jean-Léon Gérôme*, rev. ed., Paris, 2000, no. 109.

150 See, for example, Henri Delaborde, *L'Art français au Salon de 1859*, Paris, 1859, p. 101; and M. H. Dumesnil, *Le Salon de 1859*, Paris, 1859, p. 90.

151 See Gerald Ackerman, "Gérôme and Manet," *Gazette des beaux-arts*, September 1967, p. 67.

152 Dumesnil, *Le Salon de 1859*, p. 90.

153 Ackerman, *Jean-Léon Gérôme*, no. 168. Gérôme returned to the subject in 1868, copying the figure of the dead Caesar in a drawing and an etching (cited in ibid., no. 109) and adapting it for the analogous figure in his painting *The Death of Marshal Ney* (ibid., no. 170). But the latter also recalls, in the motif of the bleak stone wall, the Mannheim version of Manet's *Execution of Maximilian*, completed in the same year; see Françoise Cachin in *Manet, 1832–1883*, p. 276.

154 Charles Baudelaire, "Le Salon de 1859," *La Revue française*, June 10–July 20, 1859; as translated in *Art in Paris, 1845–1862: Salons and Other Exhibitions; Reviewed by Charles Baudelaire*,

trans. and ed. Jonathan Mayne, London, 1965, p. 176.

155 Beatrice Farwell, *Manet and the Nude: A Study in Iconography in the Second Empire*, New York, 1981, pp. 60–61 and p. 293, n. 22.

156 Alain Lesage, *Histoire de Gil Blas de Santillane. Vignettes par Jean Gigoux*, Paris, 1835, p. 56. The episode illustrated occurs near the beginning of the novel, in Book I, Chapter 9.

157 *Étudiants de Salamanque* (R-W 28), painted in 1859–60. See Proust, *Édouard Manet, souvenirs*, p. 54; the passage does not occur in the *Revue blanche* version.

158 W. S. Heckscher, *Rembrandt's "Anatomy of Dr. Nicolaas Tulp,"* New York, 1958, pp. 35–36. The corpse in Rembrandt's painting, of which Manet had painted a copy (R-W 8), is aligned more horizontally than the dead *toreador* and faces in the opposite direction and hence would not have been a source for it.

159 Wilson-Bareau, "Manet and the Execution of Maximilian," pp. 43–44 and p. 22, fig. 9. On the Poussin, see Henry Keazor, "A propos des sources littéraires et picturales de la *Peste d'Asdod*, 1630–1631, par Nicolas Poussin," *Revue du Louvre et des Musées de France*, February 1996, pp. 62–69.

160 See Pérez, in *Manet / Velázquez*, p. 459, and Mauner, *Manet, Peintre-Philosophe*, p. 138.

161 *La Chanson de Roland*, strophes clxxv–clxxvii; ed. and trans. Léon Gautier, Tours, 1872, I, pp. 187–91.

162 Michallon's *Paysage. Mort de Roland* of 1819 (Musée du Louvre) was reproduced in Charles Blanc, *Histoire des peintres de toutes les écoles. École française*, III, 1863, "Achille Etna Michallon," p. 5. On Manet's familiarity with this publication, see Theodore Reff, "Manet and Blanc's *Histoire des peintres*," *The Burlington Magazine*, July 1970, pp. 456–58.

163 On the scholarship on *La Chanson* in this period, see *La Chanson de Roland*, ed. Gautier, I, pp. clxix–clxxxvi.

164 *Catalogue d'une collection précieuse de tableaux . . . appartenant à la veuve de M. de *** [Laforest], . . . rue du Chantre, no. 24 [Paris] . . . le 7 mars 1827, no. 67*. First cited, but with an inaccurate date, in Lisa Hempel Lipschutz, *Spanish Painting and the French Romantics*, Cambridge, 1972, pp. 321–22.

165 J[ean]-J[oseph] Dubois, *Description des tableaux . . . de M. le Comte de Pourtalès-Gorgier*, Paris, 1841, p. 53. Dubois, an old acquaintance of Pourtalès's and author of the three catalogues of his collection, was a specialist in Egyptian art and assistant curator of antiquities at the Louvre. See Elisabeth Foucart-Walter, "La Rencontre d'un éminent collectionneur et d'un grand portraitiste: le *Portrait du comte de Pourtalès-Gorgier* par Paul Delaroche," *Revue du Louvre et des Musées de France*, February 2000, p. 40.

166 See the report of the expert Fleury, who was commissioned by the Louvre to examine the picture, which was then in the collection of Mme Emilie Desmolandes; Paris,

Archives des Musées nationaux, P5 1818, 29 octobre.

167 Napoleon III, *Histoire de Jules-César*, Paris, 1865, II, frontispiece. Gérôme's commission is noted in *Le Courrier artistique*, March 12, 1865, p. 164.

168 See Hillairet, *Dictionnaire historique des rues de Paris*, II, pp. 617–18.

169 See Marianne Ruggiero, "Manet and the Image of War and Revolution, 1851–1871," in *Édouard Manet and the* Execution of Maximilian, exh. cat., Brown University, Providence, 1981, p. 33.

170 Although Manet returned to Paris about June 5, 1871 (see note 171, below), after the "semaine sanglante" of May 21–28, he could have witnessed the roundups and executions that continued well beyond that week.

171 *The Barricade* (Harris 71) was probably executed in 1871 but not published until 1884. On its relation to the watercolor, see Reff, *Manet and Modern Paris*, pp. 204–7, and Wilson-Bareau in *Manet, 1832–1883*, pp. 323–26. Manet's sympathies with the Communards are attested by a letter to Berthe Morisot from her mother, June 5, 1871, cited by both authors.

172 Manet presumably saw the Goya in the Prado in 1865; and it was illustrated in a monograph published in Paris in 1867. On its relevance for different versions of his own composition, see Cachin in *Manet, 1832–1883*, pp. 273–74, and Wilson-Bareau, in ibid., pp. 277–78.

173 See "Documents Relating to the 'Maximilian Affair,'" pp. 531–34. The lithograph is H 54.

174 Émile Zola, "Coups d'épingle," *La Tribune*, February 4, 1869; as translated in "Documents Relating to the 'Maximilian Affair,'" p. 532.

175 *Civil War* (H 72), probably executed in 1871, was not published until 1874. Both the dead Caesar and the dead Orlando, themselves fallen soldiers, have also been discussed as models, but visually the dead *toreador* corresponds most closely; see Isaacson, in *Manet and Spain, Prints and Drawings*, p. 40.

176 But such is the interaction between the works of Manet and Gérôme in these years that it also recalls the bleak stone wall behind the dead figure in *The Death of Marshal Ney*, as noted by Gerald Ackerman, "Gérôme and Manet," *Gazette des beaux-arts*, September 1967, pp. 170–71.

177 Letters to Félix Bracquemond, March 18 and March 21, 1871, in Jean-Paul Bouillon, "Les Lettres de Manet à Bracquemond," *Gazette des beaux-arts*, April 1983, p. 151; as translated in *Manet by Himself*, ed. Juliet Wilson-Bareau, Boston, 1991, pp. 160–61.

178 These are, respectively, *Portrait of Rochefort*, 1881 (R-W 366); *The Escape of Rochefort*, 1881 (ibid., nos. 369 and 370); and *Portrait of Clemenceau*, 1879–80 (ibid., nos. 329 and 330).

On Manet's political portraits, see Nord, "Manet and Radical Politics," pp. 467–71.

179 This small enigmatic picture (R-W 258) has been related to Zola's account of a painter's suicide in his studio, in "Un Suicidé" at the beginning of "Mon Salon" of 1866; but in addition to being eleven years later, Manet's picture shows neither a painter nor a studio.

180 On the critical reception of *Dead Christ with Angels* (R-W 75) at the Salon, see Hamilton, *Manet and His Critics,* pp. 55–62; and on its thematic affinity with *Incident in a Bullfight,* Mauner, *Manet, Peintre-Philosope,* p. 140.

181 These are R-W 104 and 106, respectively. On the morbid content of these and other works in Manet's oeuvre, see Mauner, *Manet, Peintre-Philosophe,* pp. 110–15, and Mary Matthews Gedo, "Final Reflections: A Bar at the Folies-Bergère as Manet's Adieu to Art and Life," in *Looking at Art from the Inside Out; The Psychoiconographic Approach to Modern Art,* Cambridge, 1994, pp. 1–52.

182 It has long been thought that *The Burial* (R-W 162) was inspired by the funeral of Baudelaire in September 1867. See Nancy Locke, "Unfinished Homage: Manet's *Burial* and Baudelaire," *The Art Bulletin,* March 2000, pp. 68–82.

183 See Nancy Locke, *Manet and the Family Romance,* Princeton, 2001, pp. 44–45. Auguste Manet died on September 25, 1862.

184 *Portrait of Monsieur and Madame Auguste Manet* (R-W 30). Auguste Manet appears still more troubled in Manet's etched portrait of him, also of 1860 (H 6).

185 See Locke, *Manet and the Family Romance,* pp. 47, 56–62, and 115–18. While acknowledging that Léon's paternity remains unknown, Locke argues persuasively that it was Auguste Manet.

Fig. 1. Reconstruction by Susan Grace Galassi and Ann Hoenigswald, here modified, of the second version of Édouard Manet's *Incident in a Bullfight*. From *Manet's* The Dead Toreador *and* The Bullfight, 1999, pl. 5

Fig. 3. Henri Oulevay, caricature of Édouard Manet's *Incident in a Bullfight*. From *Le Monde illustré*, May 28, 1864

4282. JOUJOUX ESPAGNOLS ACCOMMODÉS A LA SAUCE NOIRE DE RIBERA, par DON MANET Y COURBERTOS, Y DORÉOS, Y RIBERA, Y ZUBRARAN DE LAS BATIGNOLAS.

Fig. 2. Bertall [Charles-Albert d'Arnoux], caricature of Édouard Manet's *Incident in a Bullfight*. From *Le Journal amusant*, May 21, 1864

Fig. 4. Cham [Amédée de Noé], caricature of Édouard Manet's *Incident in a Bullfight*. From *Le Charivari*, May 22, 1864

Fig. 5. Édouard Manet, *Mlle V . . . in the Costume of an Espada*, 1862. Oil on canvas, 65 x 50 ¼ (165.1 x 127.6).
The Metropolitan Museum of Art, New York; H. O. Havemeyer Collection, Bequest of
Mrs. H. O. Havemeyer, 1929

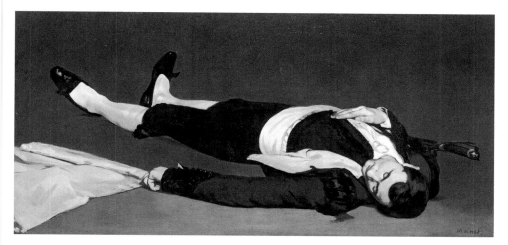

Fig. 6. Édouard Manet, *The Dead Toreador*, 1862–64. Oil on canvas, 29 ⁷/₈ x 60 ⅜ (75.9 x 153.3). National Gallery of Art, Washington, D.C., Widener Collection.

Fig. 7. Édouard Manet, *The Bullfight*, 1862–65. Oil on canvas, 18 ⁷/₈ x 42 ⁷/₈ (47.9 x 108.9). The Frick Collection, New York

Fig. 8. Édouard Manet, *Dead Toreador*, 1868. Etching and aquatint, third state, 6 ¹/₁₆ x 8 ³/₄
(15.4 x 22.1). National Gallery of Art, Washington, Rosenwald Collection

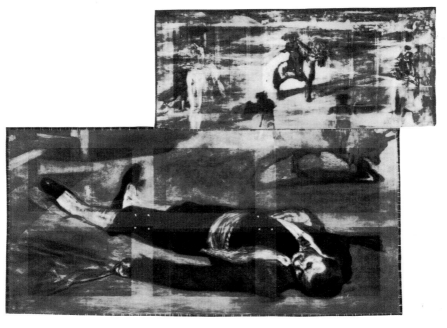

Fig. 9. Reconstruction by Theodore Reff and Ann Hoenigswald of the second version of Édouard
Manet's *Incident in a Bullfight*. From *Manet and Modern Paris*, 1982, p. 215

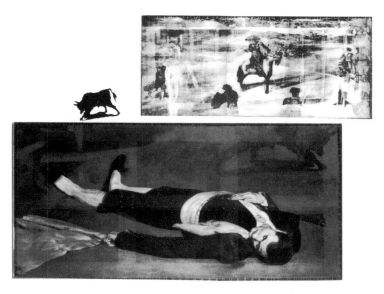

Fig. 10. Reconstruction by Susan Grace Galassi and Ann Hoenigswald of the first version of Édouard Manet's *Incident in a Bullfight*. From *Manet's* The Dead Toreador *and* The Bullfight, 1999, pl. 4

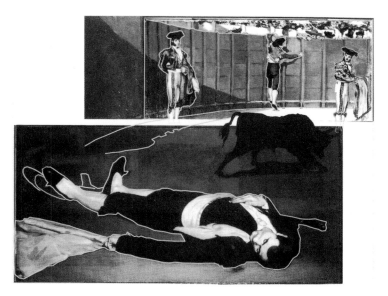

Fig. 11. Reconstruction by Susan Grace Galassi and Ann Hoenigswald of the second version of Édouard Manet's *Incident in a Bullfight*. From *Manet's* The Dead Toreador *and* The Bullfight, 1999, pl. 5

Fig. 13. Édouard Manet, *Toreadors* (formerly *The Inn*), 1862–63. Oil on canvas, 20 ¹/₂ x 35 (52 x 89). Hill-Stead Museum, Farmington, Conn., Alfred Atmore Pope Collection

Fig. 12. Gustave Courbet, *The Bullfight*, 1854–56. Oil on canvas, 18 ⁷/₈ x 22 (48 x 56). Whereabouts unknown

Fig. 14. Édouard Manet, *The Bullring in Madrid*, 1865. Oil on canvas, 35 ³/₈ x 43 ¹/₄ (90 x 110). Musée d'Orsay, Paris

Fig. 15. Édouard Manet, *The Bullfight*, 1865. Oil on canvas, 18 ⁷/₈ x 23 ³/₄ (48 x 60.4). The Art Institute of
Chicago, Mr. and Mrs. Martin A. Ryerson Collection

Fig. 16. Alfred Dehodencq, *Village Bullfight in
Spain*, 1850. Oil on canvas, 58 ⁵/₈ x 81 ¹/₈ (146 x
206). Musée des Beaux-Arts de Pau, on loan
from the Musée d'Orsay, Paris

Fig. 17. Gustave Doré, *Picador Thrown from His Horse*. Wood
engraving, 6 ¹/₄ x 9 ⁵/₈ (15.8 x 24.5). From *Le Tour du monde*,
1862. Bibliothèque nationale de France, Paris

Fig. 18. Édouard Manet, *The Dead Toreador* (detail).
National Gallery of Art, Washington, D.C., Widener
Collection

Fig. 19. *José Rodríguez (Pepete)*, before 1862. Photograph. From José María de Cossio, *Los Toros*,
1943

Fig. 20. *Bullfight and Death of Pepete*, 1862. Wash drawing. From
Lorenzo Ortiz-Cañavate, *Folklore y costumbres de España*, 1931

Fig. 21. Francisco de Goya, *The Unlucky Death of Pepe Illo in
the Ring at Madrid*, 1815–16. Etching, aquatint, drypoint, and
burin, 9 ³/₄ x 14 (24.9 x 35.5). National Gallery of Art,
Washington, D.C., Rosenwald Collection

Fig. 23. Francisco de Goya, *The Spirited Moor Gazul Is the First to Spear Bulls According to Rules*, 1815–16. Etching, aquatint, and drypoint, 9 ⅞ x 14 ⅛ (25 x 35.8). National Gallery of Art, Washington, D.C., Rosenwald Collection

Fig. 22. Franz Xavier Winterhalter, *The Empress Eugénie*, 1854. Oil on canvas, 36 ½ x 29 (92.7 x 73.7). The Metropolitan Museum of Art, New York, Purchase, Mr. and Mrs. Claus von Bülow Gift, 1978

Fig. 24. Édouard Manet, *The Dancer Mariano Camprubi*, 1862. Oil on canvas, 18 ½ x 13 (47 x 33). Private collection, United States

Fig. 25. Prince de Joinville, *Eugénie de Montijo Returning from a Bullfight at Tablada*, 1852. Watercolor, 13 x 9 ⁷/8 (33 x 25). Musée national du Château de Compiègne

Fig. 26. A.A.E. Disdéri, *Mlle Simono as a Torero*, 1861. Photograph. From Elizabeth McCauley, *A. A. E. Disdéri and the Carte de Visite Portrait Photograph*, p. 186

Fig. 27. Édouard Manet, *The Execution of Emperor Maximilian*, 1867–68. Oil on canvas, 99 1/4 x 120 (252 x 305). Städtische Kunsthalle Mannheim

Fig. 28. Italian, seventeenth century. *A Dead Soldier*. Oil on canvas, 41 ¼ x 65 ¾ (104.8 x 167). National Gallery, London

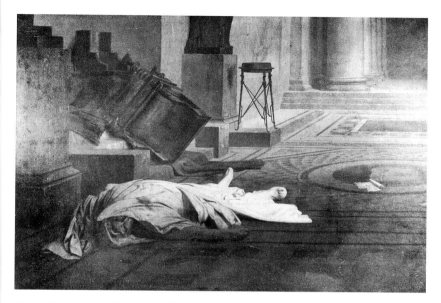

Fig. 29. Photograph of Jean-Léon Gérôme's *Dead Caesar*, 1859. Bibliothèque nationale de France, Cabinet des Estampes, Paris

Fig. 30. Jean-Léon Gérôme, *The Death of Caesar*, 1859. Oil on canvas, 33 ¹/₂ x 57 (85 x 145). Walters Art Museum, Baltimore

Fig. 31. Jean Gigoux, *Robbers Attacking a Stagecoach*. From Alain Lesage, *Histoire de Gil Blas de Santillane*, 1835. Wood engraving, 3 ³/₈ x 4 ¹/₄ (8.5 x 12)

Fig. 32. *War in Mexico, Siege and Capture of Puebla*, 1863. Pinot & Sagaire, Épinal and Paris. Colored and gilded lithograph, 10 ⅞ x 16 ⅛ (27.6 x 41). Musée national des Arts et Traditions populaires, Paris

Fig. 33. Reproduction of Achille-Etna Michallon's *Landscape. Death of Roland*. From Charles Blanc, *Histoire des peintres. École française*, 1863. Wood engraving, 5 ¼ x 6 ¾ (13.3 x 17.1). Avery Architectural and Fine Arts Library, Columbia University, New York

Fig. 34. *Group of Communards Inspecting the Toppled Statue of the Vendôme Column, May 16, 1871.* Photograph. Bibliothèque nationale de France, Paris

Fig. 35. Édouard Manet, *The Barricade*, 1871–73. Lithograph, 18 ³/₈ x 13 ¹/₈ (46.8 x 33.3). Print Collection, Miriam and Ira D. Wallach Division of Arts, Prints and Photographs the New York Public Library, Astor, Lenox and Tilden Foundations

Fig. 36. Édouard Manet, *Civil War*, 1871–73. Lithograph, 15 ³/₄ x 19 ¹⁵/₁₆ (40 x 50.7). National Gallery of Art, Washington, D.C., Rosenwald Collection, 1943

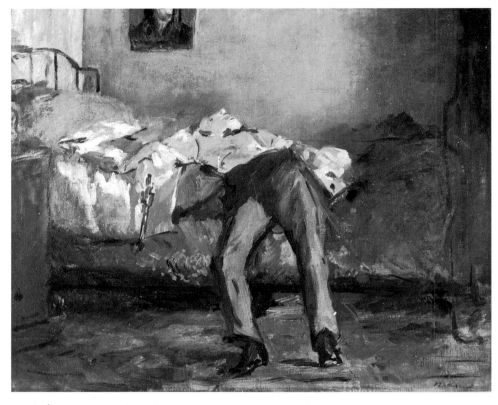

Fig. 37. Édouard Manet, *The Suicide*, c. 1877. Oil on canvas, 15 x 17 ¾ (38 x 45). Stiftung Sammlung E. G. Bührle, Zürich

Fig. 38. Édouard Manet, *Monsieur and Madame Auguste Manet*, c. 1860. Oil on canvas, 43 ⁵⁄₁₆ x 35 ⁷⁄₁₆ (110 x 90). Musée d'Orsay, Paris